Mosaic Making

Mosaic Making

Helen Hutton

LONDON: B.T.BATSFORD LTD

NEW YORK: REINHOLD PUBLISHING CORPORATION

First published 1966

Printed in Denmark by
F. E. BORDING LTD
Copenhagen and London
for the Publishers
B. T. BATSFORD LTD
4 Fitzhardinge Street
Portman Square London W 1
REINHOLD PUBLISHING CORPORATION
430 Park Avenue, New York 10022

Contents

Acknowledgment

I wish to express my thanks and great indebtedness
to the following who have given such willing help
with this book:
Jan and Zoe Ellison for technical advice on ceramics;
David Lane for glaze recipes; Tom Fairs for information on glass mosaics; Hermia and Peter Eden
for making a pavement for illustration in this book
and also for the Alhambra tile plates: Kate Varney
and the children of Cottenham Village College for
their experiments and co-operation; my son Mac-
aillan for architectural drawings of a workroom plan;
and other members of my family for their constant
goading, encouragement and practical assistance.
Finally to my son Warwick for the line drawings.

Cambridge 1966   *H. H.*

*Detail from the Santa Pudenziana Rome, dating from
the end of the fourth century*

Introduction

This book has no pretensions to being an historical survey and analysis of traditional mosaic, nor is it an attempt to discuss the aesthetic merits of the great works of the past. It is, rather, a practical approach to a craft which comes close to being an art form, on a level that may be reached by most people. Fine publications are available which have covered all aspects of world famous mosaics; it is suggested that the reader studies as many of them as are available to broaden his horizon on the whole subject.

Many new materials and techniques have arisen lately, and practical methods of applying them is the chief aim of this book. The term mosaic, therefore, is used in the broadest sense to mean an arrangement of ordered parts to form a balanced unity—and not necessarily a permanent one, as was the case with traditional mosaics. Therefore we use such materials as seeds, bark, beans, wood sections and many other impermanent tesserae and combine this multiplicity into a balanced unit.

By the use of such permanent materials as smalti, vitreous, glass, stone and marble, however, an enduring and indestructible work of art may be created in this fascinating medium.

It is hoped that much of the book will be of interest to artists who have not yet tried their hand at mosaic making, but it is also intended to reach those others who are interested in doing creative work of this kind.

By its very nature, a simple, direct approach is a necessity for mosaic making, and this is probably the reason for the success of children when designing in this medium. Their naïve vision is directly interpreted into the mosaic form.

It will be noted that quite a few of the examples shown in this book have been made by children, either as a group or individually, and the undoubted success of some of them may encourage adults who have had no art training to embark on work of this type themselves. Most of us have the child's fresh vision hidden beneath our conventional approach to art, and the manipulation of these small glowing segments of glass, stone or ceramic is the surest way to awaken it.

In the hope that this book will both teach techniques and improve aesthetic ideas, a rather lengthy chapter on design prefaces the other chapters on the various techniques, in the firmly held belief that no mosaic of any significance can be created from a poor design, and that the most faultless technique cannot mask it.

The author has assumed, perhaps arguably, that one of the greatest satisfactions in making a mosaic lies in using materials that you have either found or made yourself. Certainly this is true with children who will delight in finding unusual tesserae and making their own ceramics with clay fired by the pottery teacher. Most schools will not be fortunate enough to have their own kiln, but the examples shown of the work done by children of Cottenham Village College should prove how these facilities have enlarged and enriched their vision, under the direction of an imaginative young teacher, and it can only be hoped that other educational authorities may be sufficiently enlightened to provide such a well-equipped craft room for their children.

Finally, it should be pointed out that though mosaic making can be an expensive hobby (if you wish to equip a workshop with a kiln, etc., or if you wish to use Italian smalti exclusively) it can also be one of the cheapest. The use of stones and pebbles, bark and seeds, all of which are free for the picking, or wood segments which only have to be sawn from sticks or scraps, leaves the only expense a wood backing and the adhesive or cement.

Several examples of mosaics by well-known artists have been included in this book, but in the main the emphasis has been on smaller samples of the different techniques that may be practised by anyone with the desire to learn. Some are simple designs and methods, while others are for the more advanced or ambitious. Whatever is attempted, however, it must be remembered that it should be only the jumping off point for original work.

Design I

The place of design in relation to mosaics is of primary importance, whether it be a large mural or a small unit pattern. It is a popular misconception in this craft, as in many others, that a complete mastery of technique, combined with suitable materials, is the first requirement and fine workmanship will conceal any shortcomings of design and pattern. Without any clear understanding as to the character of the material being used, its qualities and its limitations, there is little possibility of its intrinsic beauty being realized.

A mosaic can be a dull wall cladding of a pepper and salt pattern, durable and hygienic, and can be seen in many bathrooms, cloakrooms and coffee bars used in just this way. Indeed, it is possible to buy mosaic kits which include ready-made designs, and others can be bought in the form of square paper units with the tesserae already glued on, ready for application against the prepared mortar. For those who lack interest, or confidence, or merely time, this is the obvious answer, but they can never know the deep satisfaction of designing a mosaic of their own.

It is surprising how many people possess a latent sense of form and pattern, and how many others develop it with a facility that amazes them. This pattern sense was an integral part of mankind in primitive times, as early cave-man drawings have shown us, and every succeeding civilization has produced its own type of decoration for walls, floors and many objects of everyday use. Greek, Moorish, Byzantine, Aztec, Polynesian, the highly civilized and the primitive native have all made their contribution and shown their development in this art and skill. And from the most simple and naïve outlook the finest patterns have flowered and have lived through to this day.

The pattern sense can still be found in native races and if civilization has buried it in many of us, it has not been wholly destroyed. The awareness of this is becoming apparent today as many of the old crafts are being revived, and the simple sources of their patterns and forms explored. Industry also is growing alive to the need for good design and applied decoration in this age of mechanical mass production.

The intention of this chapter is not to discuss the aesthetics of design or its historical background, but rather its practical application to mosaics.

IDEAS AND INSPIRATION FOR NON-FIGURATIVE DESIGNING

There are many ways of training the un-seeing eye to bring into focus a new world of forms, shapes and patterns that may have been invisible before. For the country dweller, the obvious sources are all around and his only problem lies in choosing the ones most suitable for his particular purpose and adapting them to a simple formula for his craft.

Nature offers an inexhaustible range of subjects: rock formations, patterns on stones, tree bark, rippling water, flint walls, seed cases, skeleton leaves or the markings on insects, butterflies or birds. Look at some of these under a magnifying glass, or better still photograph them and then enlarge sections to find their basic pattern. Cut sections of fruits or vegetables or seeds such as poppy seed

1 Repetitive motifs

heads can be adapted to form interesting motifs for design.

Those who live in towns have a less obvious, but entirely different range of inspirational sources. Here are museums rich with pattern ideas in many forms, from ceramic tiles and plates, hand-woven materials and tapestries (the borders of these have fascinating small motifs) to early wall papers, primitive jewellery and folk designs on various domestic objects. The Victoria and Albert Museum in South Kensington, London, not only has an excellent textile library, covering designs of all periods, but a very comprehensive art library which includes all aspects of mosaics, including design. It is well worth a visit.

To stimulate the imagination, pay a visit to your local junk yard or the back of a working garage, where design in a geometric form can be found in plenty among the old cogs, wheels, gear springs,

gaskets, broken sections of old bits of machinery or furniture. In chapter V some of these objects are shown in use as impressed patterns on ceramic tesserae, but they can also be used as whole units in a geometric design for such projects as pebble pavements or mosaic tiles (1). Try and find designs from the kind of things which are around you and interest you in your everyday life.

Symbols are a useful source of pattern. Various emblems, old guild seals, zodiac and heraldic emblems and Christian symbols can be translated into simple line form, enriched with added design or combined into a more intricate pattern as serves your purpose.

When outside sources from the material world fail to inspire, there are other methods by which you can create design units and shapes and by moving these around in different formations, find a pattern to your purpose. One such method is to cut a pile of

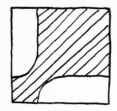
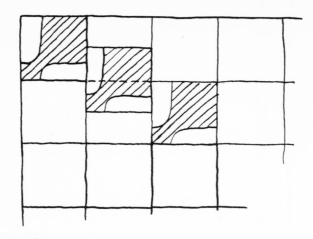

2 Half-drop motif

white or coloured paper squares, average size 2″ × 2″ or 3″ × 3″. Taking a thick crayon or chalk (a felt-tipped marker is good) draw some simple forms—diamonds, crescents, triangles, half-squares or spiral curves—the variations will be found to be innumerable. Place these alongside each other, half-drop them (2) and also use lines to connect up the motifs and try out different coloured backgrounds.

The best road to approaching design in mosaics is probably to use the material itself. It has all the qualities which make it especially suitable for falling into patterns and forms. The tesserae have a fascination which makes them irresistible both to young and old, the twinkling iridescence of their colours and the variety of their textures create the desire to handle them and move them about into groups of colour and shape and it is by doing just this that the feeling for mosaic design will gradually emerge and with it an understanding of its qualities and limitations.

When working with smalti or other small-scale tesserae, a carefully considered dark-light pattern must be combined with a broad treatment in the simple areas or a pepper and salt mosaic will result. This, unfortunately, is only too easy to achieve.

The practical method of learning the qualities of the medium is to roll out an area of modelling clay or plasticine, select a limited range of coloured tesserae and try out various placings of them on the clay. The advantage of this method is that they do not slip about, but are easily removable. Alternatively they may be laid out on a drawing board and moved around like pawns. Do sections in rectangles, triangles, curves, lay some of them flat and stand others sideways or angle them slightly. Keep the colour areas simple by using variations of one colour over an area, occasionally breaking into it with another colour to keep the surface alive.

All this time you will be learning about texture and

13

pattern as well as colour management and you might well find you prefer to leave certain areas in blank clay to form their own part in the design. These sections are sometimes called negative pattern. The use of them is clearly shown in the slab glass mosaics where the concrete between the glass chunks forms an integral part of the design (see chapter VI).

Different problems can arise with differing materials. When working with ceramics which are glazed on only one side you can get light reflection by tilting them slightly, but this is also very dependent on the surface texture of the tesserae. Commercial ceramic tesserae will probably be smooth and shiny, but the ones made by yourself can have their surface enlivened by pattern treatment which will reflect and scintillate with colour.

When using natural materials, such as stones, pebbles, shells, seeds, beans, tree bark and wood, the nature of the material will often suggest the design. The markings on wood grain or the worm-eaten lines on bark may well indicate a pattern form for the mosaic. Small shapes and more involved patterns are obviously better avoided in large-scale material and often the negative areas play their part in forming the overall design in this kind of mosaic. This is certainly applicable when using sections of bark, stones and rocks and large-scale ceramic tesserae.

These ideas apply to designing of an abstract nature, which merely means an arrangement of shapes and lines to form a balanced pattern which is pleasing to the eye. Abstract design can apply to all types of mosaics, but is especially suitable for such things as pavement units set between larger stones or concrete slabs, background walls of bathroom or patio, or smaller things like coffee tables or decorative tiles. An ordered abstract design of a wood mosaic is illustrated in chapter IX.

FIGURATIVE DESIGNING

For the figurative type of design where the medium is usually smaller-scale tesserae such as smalti, cut ceramics, commercial vitreous or seeds, the array of subjects is very wide indeed and the only deterrent may be lack of skill in translating forms from the natural world into terms of mosaic. This demands many compromises and some little experience in the fundamentals of drawing, the ability to leave out all but the most significant lines and to translate the areas of form and colour into flat pattern. It is by no means as difficult as it sounds, but though you may copy the outline of a bird or animal from a book or a picture, it must be remembered that the inner forms should be simplified into a linear design of a scale suitable to the tesserae you are using.

Almost any subject may be attempted in mosaic, from the simple rhythmic forms of plants, birds, fishes or animals to a portrait of your ideal woman—although it is not suggested that you should attempt a portrait for your first mosaic! The portrayal of the natural world in mosaic has been achieved by many artists from Byzantine times and before, and even if it is impossible to look at the originals, there are many fine books in which they can be seen and studied. Observe how the many problems have been dealt with and solved, how the colour is distributed and how contour lines describe the forms. No verbal explanations can equal the close study of a work of art. (See fig. 3 of figurative and symmetrical Graeco-Roman mosaics.)

Photography can be of great assistance in providing material for ideas as suggested earlier—rock formations, roofs of a town seen from a height, aerial photography, micro-photography of cells of plant life and sea life—all can be translated into abstract or figurative design.

3 Graeco-Roman mosaics

COLOUR AND TONE

Both of these are important factors in mosaic design, as indeed they are in any form of design, but to give any advice on colour is probably the most difficult thing in the world.

In choosing tesserae for your first mosaic, select from a limited colour range, using several tones of the same colour with one, or at the most two, contrasting colours. If you prefer to work in strong and vivid colour, avoid dotting the different colours about, but keep them in small areas with only an occasional tessera of a contrasing shade to enliven the surface. Where you have a pre-determined situation for a mosaic, it is helpful to choose one or two colours from the general scheme of decoration and allow these to predominate the design.

Working with natural material as your tesserae, the question of colour scarcely arises, as stones, pebbles, seeds, barks, etc., all have a natural mono-chromatic affinity, but when they are mixed with tile or ceramic it is better that the colour of the latter is of natural origin, (i.e. earth colours such as terracotta, yellow ochre, browns, muted greens and blues) and acid and more primary colour strictly avoided. Use varying tones of the same colour as much as possible rather than areas of exactly the same shade of colour.

Colour can, of course, be naturalistic or formalized —that is, the design can follow the natural colour of the object portrayed, such as a brown and red robin, or it can be formalized to the extent of designing the bird in blue or plain black to harmonize with a formal contrasting background. Colour need have no relation to reality for designing purposes unless you wish it to have.

The quality of colour in different types of tesserae varies a great deal and for this reason it is often better to use a mixture of several surfaces to achieve a lively mosaic. The vitreous colours are the least subtle, though amongst the wide range of rather primary shades there are also quite a few mid tints that will combine successfully with anything.

Italian smalti have the finest selection of colours obtainable: they come in many beautiful tints and half tones as well as brilliant, glowing reds, yellows, greens, blues, golds and silver, all possessing a richness of depth that is unequalled in any other form of tessera.

Cut tesserae from stained glass has a quality of its own, but its full beauty can only be appreciated when backed by white plaster of Paris or silver leaf.

TEXTURE AND REFLECTION

These should be given great consideration in a good mosaic. In the heavier natural materials like wood, bark and stones, reflection is absent and the part played by texture is even more important. The placing of stone beside stone, flat, sideways, upended, ridged by small pebbles perhaps; or again tesserae of the smalti variety, bevelled faces, lines and areas of upended or side-placed smalti, all make their contribution towards a surface of shimmering reflection. The home-made ceramics with their faces embossed with various texture patterns to break and reflect light into a myriad coloured facets, make of a mosaic a living thing with ever-changing aspects from each line of vision.

Contrasting texture, by placing a matt earthenware tessera beside a glittering glazed one, is a treatment that should be exploited.

Larger natural material, sections of different toned and grained woods and barks should bring a feeling for texture into full play. Many kinds of barks and wood should be collected with as varied surfaces as possible, seeds with wrinkled and pitted skins and the glossy purple skinned beans to combine with lichen green bark or the rich chocolate glow of coffee beans. Combining rough with smooth is usually very successful (see chapter VII).

FORM AND REPETITION

The organization of shapes and forms into a repetitive pattern is one of the earliest manifestations of designing and can be seen in nearly all primitive art. Some of its most lively examples today can be seen in the woven pulp tapa cloths from the Pacific Islands, and from Javanese and African carving and weaving. All these show repetition in its simplest form and the message is clear to read.

A retrospective journey through civilizations show us the pattern-making of Ancient Greece and early Egypt giving examples of a form (which may in itself be quite insignificant) repeated to become a rich design, still in use today. The Byzantine and Moorish periods have also left an indelible mark in this field, as the illustrations of the Alhambra tiles will reveal (4), and from all these may be seen how the force of design is accentuated when a motif is repeated, reversed, turned and repeated in reverse. The dark-on-light and light-on-dark repeats contribute largely to this type of pattern, combined with the negative spaces left between the motifs.

4 *Alhambra tiles*

The understanding of this element in design is an essential factor in pavement, patio or courtyard mosaics. Study the sets of repetitive motifs in the illustrations and notice how many variations can be worked out from them (1). Countless examples will

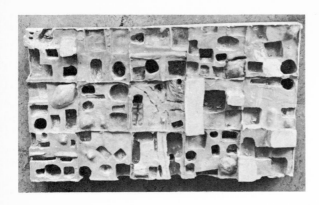

5 Concave-convex design in plaster

ing, Greek and Roman pavements, as well as many modern printed fabrics.

Practical ways of bringing about contrast is mosaics are as follows: The use of a different toned grout is sometimes sufficient to explain the main outline of a shape and where cracks are left between one form and another the demarcation may be sufficiently shown. A strong change of tone will bring about contrasted form just as successfully as a change of colour, while the use of two different colours of the same tone value might be ineffectual.

No advice can be as valuable as working and playing with the material itself, placing and replacing areas of light and dark until the feel of the right depth of contrast arrives.

FUNCTION, DIMENSION AND SCALE

The above factors are closely interrelated. Dimension and scale are more dependent upon the kind of mosaic required, and its situation, than are some of the other factors already referred to; though a unification of all of them is the obvious ideal.

To give an exaggerated example of this principle in practice: envisage a design of a small fish motif as a decorative tile and then the same design in the same ratio on the wall of a large patio. A monster of horror would probably result, out of all proportion to its situation and surroundings, while the fish on a small tile for a fireplace surround would be in a scale harmonious with its setting.

The subject chosen, abstract, figurative or merely pattern, depends directly on its relationship to the size of the tesserae and to the overall size of the mosaic. To use 1″ tesserae in a mosaic of 4″ × 4″ is clearly impossible unless an extremely simple motif of geometric origin is made.

All this may seem too obvious to stress, but it is

be discovered and a stimulating lesson in design will have been learnt. (See fig. 5, which is a plaster model of cubes and circles in concave and convex pattern.)

There is a constant need to retreat and observe the forms and shapes from a distance, or from above, if possible, especially where a floor or pavement or any large-scale mosaic is the subject. It is sometimes possible to lay the designed cartoon on a flat surface out of doors and view it from an upstairs window, or to place it on the floor of the hall and look at it from the top of the stairs. Even standing on a table or the top of a ladder is invaluable for viewing a mosaic objectively and forming an assessment of the repetitive pattern values, and indeed, its whole strength as a design.

Contrast, another factor which applies to all designing, is the means by which the dark-light balance in a pattern is brought about; the principles of it should be appreciated and understood by the mosaic artist.

The plainest example of contrast is probably the chess board and the many variations of alternating light and dark seen in primitive weaving, batik printall too common to find a student confronted with an array of large chunky ceramic tesserae, preparing to do a portrait head or a figure where certain concessions to realism are necessary but will be impossible to achieve owing to the size of the tesserae. Even if these are cut and shaped the medium is out of scale with the subject.

Rocks, stone and bark are best used on fairly large-scale projects where their rough texture and rather massive nature is seen at its best set in thick ciment fondu or ordinary concrete, the mortar forming its part of the design with its negative spaces.

A random design (i.e. the type of design in which the tesserae are moved about in a haphazard manner until a balanced pattern results) is the best for this kind of mosaic, and one of the most successful I have ever seen was an enormous head of a bull done by a first-year art student. The materials used were large sections of broken tiles, flower pots, slates and a few specially fired ceramic tesserae that were shaped to form certain areas of the head and neck, but they were perfect in scale for the subject and size of the work.

Practical requirements must be remembered when designing for a specific purpose. Flat non-porous tesserae should be used when the surface will need frequent cleaning or has to stand up to footsteps. Common sense should prevail here.

Outdoor projects will demand a different treatment as well as another technique, weather-proof tesserae and a mortar that is both water and frost proof. Pavements that are in constant hard use should be laid reasonably flat although it is quite common to lay pebbles sideways, packed closely together, as they bed down into the concrete better this way and can have flat paving units between each section. Avoid such fragile material as glazed ceramics, shells or thin glass (this always looks wrong out of doors).

Small seeds, beans, etc., are ideal materials for small-scale decorative panels, and although they lend themselves well to pattern designs they are also very suitable for subject mosaics, using such forms as a fish, a bird, a reptile, a butterfly, the head of a small animal or indeed anything of a scale to fit comfortably into the area of the panel. (See fig. 141 where a woodpecker has been worked in seeds.)

Some will prefer to find subjects from things in everyday use or more conventional motifs.

METHODS AND PROBLEMS IN DESIGNING

How actually to begin a mosaic is a problem for many people. There are several methods of approach, but a few basic rules are common to all of them.

The decisions to be made are: what is the mosaic to be for? Merely a decorative panel or for some practical use such as a sundial, a table top or a pavement? Secondly, where is it to go? Thirdly, what type of tesserae to use? When these decisions have been made, the kind of design appropiate for all these considerations must be assessed.

The need for simplicity in the case of a beginner must be stressed again. For a first attempt start by doing a small tile with a design of a geometric form, or a figurative one of a fish or scallop shell, limited to two or three colours but using as many shades of these colours as possible. If you are thinking of covering a small section of wall, perhaps round a sink or a fireplace, try and decide upon a motif that will repeat well and harmonize with the surroundings. If, on the other hand, you want to embark on a larger design to cover an area of wall as a single mural, then a drawing must be worked out beforehand and enlarged to the size required by squaring out a cartoon. (See fig. 7 and description of the method for working below.) This should be placed on the wall and carefully and thoughtfully considered before the actual mosaic is started.

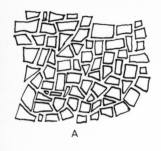

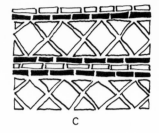

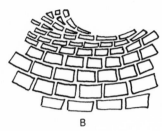

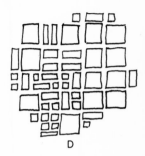

6 Ways of laying tesserae

If the Reverse method is to be used (see chapter IV) a lot of preliminary experimentation should take place before the unit sections are finally glued with tesserae and applied to the wet mortar.

If the Direct method is used, the tesserae must be selected and tried out in very much the same way, but left in their final position on the cartoon before being placed individually in position into the prepared mortar. These methods are described in chapters III and IV.

At this stage, while the tesserae are being moved about and positioned, the effects of differing textures should be observed, as this is just as important as colour in the finished mosaic. Try out the effect of the same colour in different types of tesserae—for example, a blue in smalti, stained glass, ceramic tile used right way up and in reverse, or encaustic tile.

METHOD OF LAYING TESSERAE

The contour line—the line of direction taken by the tesserae in describing the form, is another factor in their design potential.

They can be laid in many ways: placed haphazard, following the contour line, placed according to the pattern or placed in a rectangular manner as bricks are laid (6). Different sized tesserae contribute to liveliness of design.

The method used for laying the tesserae is dependent firstly on the kind of design—whether it is a figurative subject, a random type of design or a pattern—and secondly on the size of the mosaic and the type of tesserae you want to use. Look at the various examples shown in the different chapters and observe the many approaches to this problem and how widely the solution differs according to the material used.

The use of negative space, as discussed earlier, forms its part in the contour pattern, sometimes by the cracks left between the mortar following the lines of direction, while sometimes the use of a dark coloured grout has the effect of throwing the lighter toned tesserae areas into a stronger relief.

The beginner will be wise to limit the materials used in the first mosaic to those from one source, and only attempt to relate them to several others when more experience has been gained.

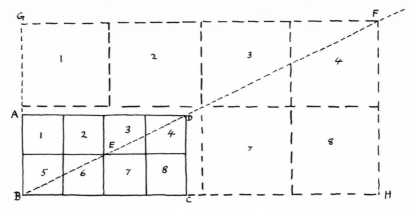

A METHOD OF ENLARGING A SMALL SKETCH TO A WORKING SIZE CARTOON

It is essential that the final size shall be in the same proportion as the sketch. The following method shows how to do this without any complicated mathematics or measuring.

In diagram 7 the sketch is assumed to be the rectangle ABCD on the bottom left hand corner. The enlarged size is the rectangle BGFH, the enlargement being shown in dotted lines. All you have to do is to draw a diagonal through the sketch from point B to point D and extend it to point F, which will be the diagonal of the finished project. You then extend the base line BC to a point H which is cut by a vertical dropped from point F. Next draw the line BA to a point (G) which is again an exact horizontal from point F. You then have a rectangle in exact proportion to your sketch, always assuming that your sketch has been outlined as a perfect rect-

angle. You next divide the sketch, first in halves and then in quarters and do the same on the full-scale one. You can go on dividing up into as many squares as you like, providing both rectangles get the same treatment. These small squares will enable you to copy your design very easily, by using the numbers which correspond on each rectangle.

On a large-scale project it is useful to use a felt ink-marker (of which many types are on the market) or a $1/2''$ badger brush and ink to ensure that the outline to be followed will be bold and clear. If it has to be traced on to the working surface or another board, use carbons sellotaped together to the required size, and then re-draw the lines more strongly in brush and ink.

In random designing it will probably be necessary merely to lay out a provisional grouping of the material, shifting pieces about until a balanced mosaic falls into place. It is then transferred from the designing board to its final placing, bit by bit.

In the various examples which come under different chapter headings, individual designs are discussed in more detail than is possible here.

Workplace, Equipment and Materials   II

It seems obvious to start a book on mosaic making with some ideas on *where* to make them, before embarking on *how* to make them and becoming submerged in the approach to the various techniques. Most people will have to make do with the limited space that can be made available in the house and this will probably be adequate if a large work bench or stout table can be provided. Generally this is better made at a height for standing, as a great deal of work involves moving about; and bending over the mosaic from a height can be a backbreaking affair.

For the times when you can sit down, or when children want to work, high stools can be provided. This bench should be as near the source of daylight as possible, avoiding it coming from such an angle as to cause a disturbing reflection from certain types of tesserae—glazed ceramics or glittering stained glass could do this. Direct sunlight is to be avoided.

If artificial light is to be used, as it must be for the many people who will work at night, a diffused source coming from a light strip is the best form of illumination, as it casts no shadows. It is now pos-

8 Jars of tesserae

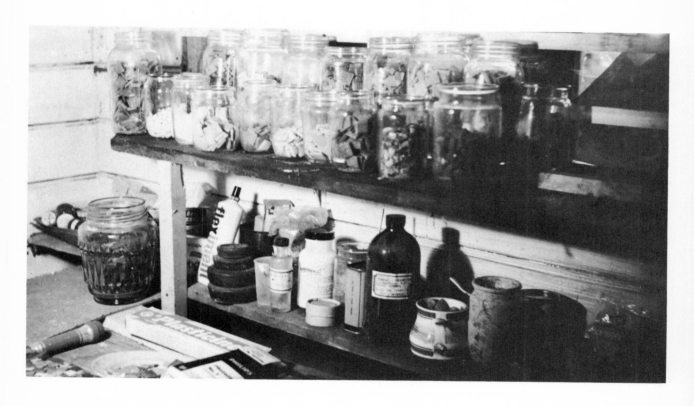

sible to buy colour-balanced fluorescent strip lighting, (or mix with tungsten lighting in the proportions of 3 fluorescent to l tungsten) and this is a great assistance when choosing and matching colours.

A large cupboard, or failing this ample shelf space,

is essential for keeping the jars of tesserae (8 and 9) the tools, cement, glues, grouts and general equipment. If these have to be kept out of doors, they should be in a dry frost-proof shed.

The availability of a sink and running water is

very important, especially when you wish to make your own mortars, or work with home-made ceramics. When a special room or an outside shed or a barn can be made available for a studio, the possibilities are much greater and more provision both for working and equipment can be considered.

A suggested plan for a good working layout for this workroom is shown (10) but the average person will obviously have to modify this considerably, depending on the size of the space available and the amount to be spent (11).

Side 1 of the workroom should be used for designing and for cartoons. It could be covered with some insulating board suitable for pinning up drawings, sketches, reproductions which may provide inspiration or even the actual things themselves: bits of bark, sections of seed pods, cogs and various natural forms.

Side 2 can be lined with storage shelves for jars of tesserae, stones, pebbles, all the various materials that may be used (9). These should be above at eye level, with a bench beneath for general sorting out into colour groups and setting the chosen colours into open dishes. Below this there could be racks for storing drawing paper, tracing paper, lining paper (for backing cement panels, described in chapter VI) and general rough work. If stained glass is used it could also be stored here where it is pulled out for checking the colours.

Side 3 should house the heavy-duty workbench with a pottery sink in a convenient position. The shelves above would take the smaller containers of glues and general adhesives, cement colours, etc., while racks and hooks would be provided for carpentry tools and mortar tools and general tools.

On this side all general carpentry for frame making would take place, the cutting of reinforcing wire and the mortar mixing. Storage cupboards beneath would hold cement, sand, lime, expanded metal, etc. Where ceramic mosaics are to be made on a large scale it will be necessary to provide space to store

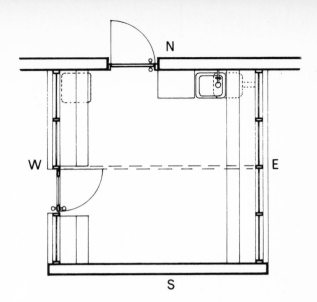

10 *Ground plan of workroom*

clay, slips, glazes and install a small kiln for the firing of them. This will be discussed under the heading of ceramic mosaics and glass fusing.

Two tables are really essential: one large heavy one for constructing the mosaics, preferably on rollers, and a smaller one to be used for smaller mosaics or for holding the saucers of tesserae when working on a large project.

The fourth side of the room will probably have the door, and the space on either side can be used for countless other storage purposes that will become necessary as you progress. A bookshelf containing technical and reference books, and wood stored on racks could also be stored here if space was not available on side 3.

There are many different types of mosaics and as many technical methods of making them, most requiring different equipment, so it will simplify matters to list the tools and materials needed under the methods described. Certain basic requirements are listed below that will be used for most carpentry and cement mixing.

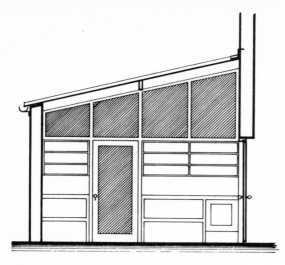

11 Elevation of workroom—west wall

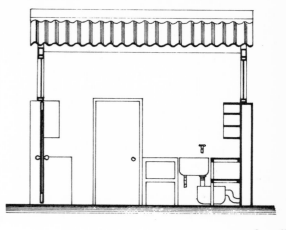

—north wall

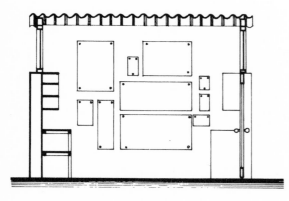

—south wall

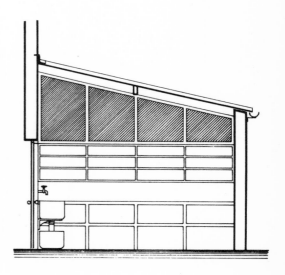

—east wall

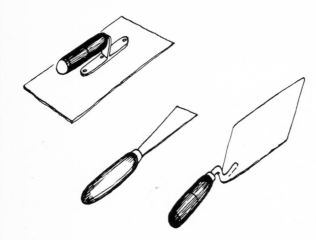

12 Some mortar equipment

EQUIPMENT

Carpentry

A hammer, a saw, pliers, pincers, screwdrivers, a drill and various sized bits, a set square, a steel rule, a good selection of screws and nails. A vice is not a necessity, but very useful.

Cementing

A mixing board made from 1″ deal boards joined closely by wooden battens: 3′ × 3′ is a good size. Alternatively a mix can also be done in a galvanised wheelbarrow (which must be *thoroughly cleaned* afterwards). Small quantities can be done in a shallow enamelled basin. Several measures are useful, a laying-on trowel, spreading knives, palette knives, grouting squeegees and large tweezers.

Clay work and glazing (13)

A roll of scrim or sacking to roll the clay on or a large plaster batt which can be purchased from a pottery firm.

Scales for measuring glaze materials. Postal scales will serve, but a pair that will measure grammes is a great advantage for accuracy with glaze ingredients.

A pestle and mortar for grinding down glazes.

Sieves, 120 mesh is the size most generally required.

Rollers for rolling out the clay. These can be wooden, but a wine bottle will serve equally well.

Several wooden battens for checking the thickness of the clay.

Knives, palette knives, badger or fitch paint brushes, small sponges for smoothing the clay surface.

In addition a large flat photographic developing-dish for holding slips and glazes is useful.

13 Ceramic equipment

14 Three different types of tesserae

MATERIALS

Tesserae

The traditional materials of the mosaic artist are the small, opaque glass cubes, square or rectangular, known as smalti. Of Italian origin, these are grouped together to form a design or pattern which makes up the mosaic. *Tessera* (singular) is Latin for square piece and *tesserae* is the plural of this.

By far the finest quality of these tesserae on the market today are the Italian smalti, Venetian glass tesserae which are made by a factory that has been working by this traditional method for centuries. Indeed, most of the world-famous mosaics to be seen in Italy today are made of smalti.

The small rectangles (approx $\frac{1}{2}'' \times \frac{3}{4}''$) are by no means cut level and this varying uneven surface gives them a reflective glitter that has a jewel-like quality. They come in a colour range that covers the complete spectrum and have a beauty and richness possessed by no other mosaic medium. They are, however, rather expensive, prohibitively so if used exclusively on a large scale, but mixed with stained glass tesserae or vitreous tesserae, can be almost as effective and the cost will be considerably less. The prices of individual colours vary widely, but in general the earth colours (terracotta, yellow ochre, burnt umber) are the cheapest, and the gold and silver the most costly.

Some of the earlier mosaics were made of even smaller tesserae ($\frac{1}{4}'' \times \frac{1}{4}''$) when a design confined to very minute detail was required. Even smaller ones were called *filato* (thread), the tesserae being formed by cutting sections of a long thread-like rod. A great deal of jewellery and highly detailed mosaics were made by this method, the tesserae being set in place by tweezers and often constructed under a magnifying glass. Very little of this work is done

15 Ceramic kiln (Podmore's)

today, but some fine examples can be seen in the antique jewellery section at the Victoria and Albert Museum in London. (For those who are interested in this kind of work, a method for making the Filato Mosaics can be found in *The Art of Mosaic Making* by Jenkins and Mills, D. Van Nostrand, New Jersey, U.S.A.)

VITREOUS TESSERAE

These are of opaque glass used widely for commercial projects, coffee bars, shop fronts, kitchens, bathroom and many decorative mosaics. They come in ³/₄″ squares and can be bought loose by the pound or glued to 1 foot square sheets of paper. The shades are inferior to the smalti and the colour range very much more limited. They are however considerably cheaper and can be cut quite easily with tile nippers into four smaller squares, narrow strips or diagonals, the glass being much thinner than the smalti. Their reflective value is rather poor.

Ceramics

HOME-MADE

These are possibly some of the most interesting tesserae that can be used. They can be glossy and reflective or have a dull but glowing matt texture, depending on the glazes used. After the initial expense of the necessary equipment (which can be considerable if the cost of a kiln is included) these are about the cheapest tesserae that can be used. They can be made in any size or thickness or shape, tailored to the design in fact; and the colours can be of your own choosing, dependent of course on your success with the glazes.

The method for making them is fully described in chapter V, and the necessary equipment is listed. Suppliers for materials can be found in the list at the end of the book. The type of kiln necessary is described and shown in fig. 15.

16 Broken china

COMMERCIAL

Commercial ceramics, usually in the form of tiles, are either glazed or encaustic. In the case of the former the glaze is laid on the pre-fired (biscuited) clay and the colour, obtained by oxides and dependent on the temperature of the firing, is on the surface only. Tiles are brighter and more diverse in colour but are not proof against the weather and are unsuitable for outdoor conditions. Small varieties can be bought but they are more usually in the 4″ × 4″ size which must be cut or shaped with a tile nipper.

The encaustic ones, which are considerably more limited in colour, are practically impervious to weather and are used for outdoor conditions, wall surfaces, floors and pavements. All the early Roman mosaics were made of tiny encaustic tesserae.

In the manufacture of these, either the colour of the clay itself or the pigment which is mixed with the clay before firing, decides the colouring, and the tile being solid colour throughout is very durable.

The colours, however, are earth colours, whether made from natural clay or with oxides, so the tones are dull and subdued—browns, greys, terracotta (red earth), yellow ochres. They can be combined very attractively with pebbles and stones, having a close relationship in their colour and texture.

Other ceramic material of more humble origin are broken flowerpot pieces, broken china collected by yourself and your friends (16).

Incidentally, one of the most pleasant little paved patios I have seen was made by an old lady who had collected her breakages of a lifetime and set them in a little circular pavement outside her cottage door. The china bits had been selected rather carefully, blue willow-pattern predominating, and an original spiral design had been used relating the blues and greys of the Wedgwood with the other colours and patterns to form circles. It is unfortunate that no photograph was ever taken of this.

17 Slab glass

18 Slab glass panel

Glass

Although both smalti and vitreous tesserae come under the heading of glass, stained glass and clear glass and slab glass is also used in mosaic making. The materials and equipment will be listed in the technique section.

STAINED GLASS

This can be bought in sheets from stained glass firms and can often be bought as offcuts, bits and pieces that are too small for the use of stained glass artists. Various qualities and thicknesses of the glass are available and almost all will serve for the mosaic artist, although some are very much harder or more brittle than others. The 'flashed' (colour fused on to one side only) is the hardest and should only be cut on the unflashed side. Colourless glass can be backed with colour or affixed to stained sections. Glass filaments can sometimes be obtained or cut.

The tesserae made from stained glass can be used alone on a white base so that the colour glows, or it can be mixed with other tesserae where all except the very pale colours read as black.

SLAB GLASS

This glass is imported mainly from France in thick slabs of an average size of $8'' \times 12'' \times 1''$ thick (17). It has a wide range of colours and for large orders can be supplied in any shade required. A great number of artists, however, buy the clear glass and glue stained glass over this to make the colour required, using a transparent adhesive. This reduces the cost of the selenium shades, which are very expensive, but you must accept the fact that any mosaic requiring slab glass in large quantities will be very costly. Used with a concrete base as shown (18) a relatively small amount of glass is needed and the concrete plays an important part in the design.

The slab glass mosaic is usually designed over a light box, illuminated from below with a strip light. When the design is finally determined it is transferred to a cartoon for the cementing. A full description of a mosaic done by this process is to be found in chapter VI.

19 Tray of mosaic pebbles

BOTTLE GLASS

This can be collected either on the beaches or at home. The seashore glass is generally worn and sanded down by the breaking waves and can be used just as it comes.

Wine bottles or other interesting glass must be broken up carefully. They may either be covered with sacking or placed inside several paper bags and then hammered. Gloves should be worn for this job.

The circular bases of wine bottles can be collected to make a mosaic and if several shades of greens and browns are selected, the result has a quite individual charm. When the bottle is broken, the base usually falls free, but if any further hammering has to be done an eye shield should be worn. Another method is to pour boiling water into the bottle.

The fusing of both the stained and bottle glass in a kiln is fully described in chapter VI.

Pebbles, stones, flints and fossils

These are the basic materials for some of the most attractive mosaics. Those who live in cities are generally able to buy these from sand and gravel merchants or garden suppliers, but for the average person the pleasures of collecting these at the seaside or at the local gravel pits is incomparably more exciting and rewarding (19).

Searching and finding on beaches and in quarries gives a purpose to expeditions and all the family, down to the smallest child, can join in this pursuit.

If you want to collect systematically, you should give each member of the party a plastic bag and instructions to find a certain colour or size. Living in East Anglia I have found the coast of Norfolk a treasure ground in varieties, colours and shapes, and the East coast from Walton-on-Naze to beyond

Most large towns have a geological museum where specimens of the local rocks and stones are shown together with the sites of the quarries. Alternatively the Geological Museum in South Kensington, London, gives full coverage to the geological areas of England, Scotland and Wales, showing the quarries and types of rock outcrops in each county. The United States of America is, of course, a much richer country in minerals and semi-precious stones, and among the best hunting grounds are California and Colorado. Here also booklets on the areas can generally be obtained quite easily.

The situations in which stones and pebbles may be used are many. Outdoor projects can be enlivened by them—panels set into brick or stone walls, patios, pavements, the paving of ponds, garden tables and benches. With imagination they can be used on indoor sites: mantlepiece surrounds, hearth paving, panels behind sinks or cookers, these especially in country cottages in areas where such stones and pebbles are plentiful. See the illustrations in chapter VII.

Shells

Generally speaking, shells are not a very successful material for making mosaics. From the design standpoint they tend to look arty-crafty and it can be difficult to escape from this aspect. From the practical angle they are often too fragile and unless bedded-down well into the cement are easily broken. They seldom present a sufficiently flat surface for the use of a glue adhesive, and even when they can be successfully glued, are very often knocked off. It is possible, however, to make a purely decorative picture with them, made within a frame to hang on the wall, where they will look charming and collect a good deal of dust. Children often delight in making shell mosaics, and if allowed to experiment with this medium can be kept amused for hours.

Yarmouth is equally good. All the beaches around the coast have a fine selection of pebbles and rich sources of semi-precious stones can be found in many quarries and gravel pits. Fossils also abound in many of these. The purpose of this book, however, is to instruct in mosaic making, so I have merely given a brief summary of the stones and pebbles to be found around the coast and refrained from making a geological survey of the whole country! The collection of interesting pebbles is a fascinating hobby and the question of what to do with them when you have brought them home may find an answer in the making of a mosaic.

If you live inland and in region where there are quarries, such as Anglesea, Derbyshire, Wales, Cumberland, Cornwall, Westmorland or Pembrokeshire, many fascinating rocks and minerals can be found, such as fluorspar, barytes, quartz (the various marbles).

Iridescent furnace slag, which is a greenish-blue and not actually a mineral, can be found in many industrial areas and in quantities around the Ironstone Valley near Much Wenlock in Shropshire.

Many varieties of shells can be used and here again the beaches are the main source of supply and the hunt a part of the pleasure. It is possible to buy shells of the exotic tropical kind from shell shops if you cannot collect your own. The more simple shapes such as oysters, mussels and cockles can be combined successfully with stones and ceramics, but the more fussy varieties are seldom successful used in this way (20).

The example illustrated (21) of a square mosaic plaque is made from black and white stones, commercial tesserae and cowrie shells. These shells are used face downwards throughout most of the design, as will be seen, but at certain points were laid on their backs—the open line down the middle making a more interesting pattern.

The following shells can be found on various beaches in England and are all suitable for mosaics. A much wider selection can be found on warmer parts of the Atlantic coast and a few are mentioned here.

Saddle oyster
Limpet
Whelk
Mussels (varieties)
Top (varieties)
Cockle
Scallop (varieties)
Astarte (varieties)
File
Tellin
Venus shell
Sand caper
Razor
Mail shells
Ormer or sea ear (St Malo)
Winkles (varieties)
Wentletrap
Cowries (southern Atlantic)

20 *Three types of shells*

As no example is available to supply details of the technique, the following is a brief résumé as to the best way to use shells. After you have collected a supply for mosaic work they should be scrubbed, dried and sorted into boxes, grading into both shapes and sizes. Any type of plywood or composition board can be used as a base provided it is at least $1/4''$ thick or, if a large mosaic is planned, battened on the back to prevent warping.

Shells are delicate decorative type of material to work with and this should be remembered when making the design. The lines and shapes should be kept simple and planned in areas as the shells themselves will provide pattern and texture. Colour will only be a consideration to a limited extent as the

range is in tone more than in shade. Some lovely deep blues are found in the mussels and there are many pastel pinks in the scallops. However, the main shades are greys, browns, whites, creams, with various stripes and mottles that provide lively patterns. (See fig. 150 page 121 for a mosaic combining oyster shells and bark.)

They can be glued on to a previously coloured base with one of the many adhesives such as *Unibond, Evostick, Bostik*. The base can also be the plain wood or composition board. Concave shells which cannot be stuck flat must have the hollow filled with a fine cement (see chapter XI) or a compound like *Nic-o-Bond Thikbed* and when set, the glue is applied to this.

Alternatively the base can be a cement bed or a *Nic-o-Bond Thikbed* mix into which they are embedded deeply enough to be held down securely.

The framing of these shell mosaics should be considered carefully. Often a rather fussy Victorian frame becomes the ideal surround, but nearly always the frame should be deeply recessed; firstly because the 'looking into' feeling enhances the evocative quality of the shells and secondly for the more practical reason that the mosaic is less likely to be knocked and broken than it would be on a flat surface. Wide ribbon velvet glued round the frame makes a pleasing setting. A deeply recessed frame can also be glazed, as protection against dust.

Seeds, beans, bark and other natural objects

These materials are very popular with children for work in schools and also as a home occupation. In country areas the seeds, beans or indeed any natural objects that take the eye can be collected over the summer and into the autumn, dried, baked and stored, or used at once if inspiration is there. People living in towns will find a surprising variety in the everyday beans and pulses used for cooking, and the continental delicatessen will probably show many more unfamiliar types. If you live in London, Soho is the place to visit.

As a material they are cheap to buy and free for the finding in the country, and rambles in lanes, on heaths and moors can be enriched if your eye is alert for useful material for your mosaics. Many trees have seeds and pods as well as bark in a great range of hues and textures. The plants in your garden, both vegetables and flowers, will make their contribution.

In chapter VIII a more detailed list of materials can be found together with the methods for using them, and several examples of this kind of mosaic. (See chapter X for seed mosaic masks.)

Other materials

Many other materials may be discovered and used by the perceptive and original, and children probably form the largest group in this class. 'Tesserae' I have seen collected by them include fish backbones, skeletons or small animals found in the fields, metal tops from mineral bottles, sections of knots from trees, marbles, etc.

Cut or torn paper, or cut sections of cotton and wool material are popular in schools to make a glued patchwork mosaic that has a very naïve charm and quality. An example of this is shown and described in chapter IX.

Wood in the form of sea-silvered driftwood, or the scraps of waste found in the pile at a timber yard or in the waste bin give other interesting materials to the mosaic artist. It is more colourful than one would imagine—purple brown, silver grey, light cream and golden tan, and can be artificially bleached or stained if the natural tone does not please. Pieces may be found that are textured with ancient worm-holes, general decay or wear from wind and sea. How to prepare and make these mosaics is also to be found in chapter IX.

The materials generally used for the many decorative objects in daily use, such as coffee tables, plant tables, serving trays, fruit plates, cheese boards, bread boards, teapot tiles, bird baths, etc., are usually the commercial tesserae or smalti.

They should always be set in a firm mortar of 3 parts sand to 1 part cement, and whether the Direct or Reverse method is used, given a final grouting to ensure that the surface will not collect dirt and can be easily cleaned. No small objects have been treated individually in this book, as they are all readily obtainable from craft shops ready for decoration by mosaics, and the various methods will be described fully in later chapters.

The Direct Method III

This is the oldest and at the same time the most straightforward technique, as its name suggests—the placing of the tesserae on to a base which can be either a vertical or a horizontal surface; the setting agent being a cement mortar, or alternatively some type of glue adhesive.

It has several aesthetic advantages over the Indirect or Reverse method, the outstanding one being that a more variable surface texture can be created by using different kinds of tesserae, in a wider range of sizes and shapes. The fact that these can be individually placed and tilted on different angles by hand gives a reflecting surface of light and shadow. Some may be laid flat, others sideways or angled, giving the mosaic a scintillating vitality, unsurpassed by any other method.

The skilled craftsman can combine many materials —smalti, ceramics, stained glass, or pebbles and sections of wood, all of which give a more free vein to expression than is possible by indirect means.

By use of the Reverse method this surface vitality is to a large extent lacking, a certain fresh quality is inevitably lost and a mosaic which goes beyond the limitations of a craft is usually one done by the Direct method. The advantages of the Reverse method are for the most part on the practical side, when a whole mosaic mural has to be prepared beforehand in transportable units, and this is discussed in detail in chapter IV.

The Direct method was the one employed in the early traditional mosaics during the Byzantine empire and there are several surviving examples to be found in Greece and Italy. Some smaller ones, which can be seen in the original form in the British Museum in London, are shown in chapter I, as they are accessible to the many who are unable to see the more famous ones at Ravenna, Rome, Pompeii, Florence, Venice, and many others in Greece.

This was the sole method in use until the end of the thirteenth century when mosaics reached their finest peak and the need to mass-produce them became apparent. Well-known mosaic artists employed journeymen in their studios who would pre-assemble a whole mosaic by glueing it on to paper sections, and thus complete a large work under the personal supervision of the master. Under the earlier system, the journeymen had worked instead for long periods on the site, and the very act of laying each tessera individually into the mortar had lent to the mosaic that vitality which we recognize today.

Working in this way, the tessera was laid direct into the wet mortar. In the method used most widely today, the tessera is glued onto a plaster or hardboard surface, and afterwards grouted, although many prefer the early method when using media of differing thickness.

The procedure for the mortar-bedded mosaic is briefly as follows: For a large-scale mural, the design is drawn out and then divided into suitable sized units by the method of scaling out as described in chapter I.

A tracing is made of each of these units, which are one by one transferred to the wet mortar sections on the wall, remembering that the thickness of this setting bed is determined by the size in depth of the largest tessera. Re-trace the guide lines with a tailor's wheel or a sharply pointed probe. The average setting time of a mortar is 2 to 3 hours, so if a detailed design involving the use of small tesserae is to be done, a smaller area of setting bed should be laid. See chapter XI for the recipe for this setting bed.

The next step is to lay on the tesserae which are transferred from the original cartoon and set, one by one, along the guide lines in the mortar, pressing them well in. It is obvious that the mortar must not be too wet or the tesserae will become submerged. The amount of pressure must be carefully gauged as if it is insufficient they will fall out and if they are pushed in too far they will drown. Use tweezers to pick out any submerged tesserae and wash to clean off mortar before replacing.

On the completion of a section, wash away any surplus mortar to leave a clean edge before starting the next section. Damp the set mortar at the junction before the next lot is applied against it. This technique is very fully described on pages 40–6.

If a portable type of mosaic is required, as it may be in a situation where conditions are such that it is not possible to work on the site, units may be prepared beforehand, and set into the prepared wall, which is usually corbelled out to receive it. These units should not be larger than 2′ × 2′ as beyond this they are difficult to handle and attach to the wall. Backing boards are required which are removed when the mortar has set and metal reinforcing is an essential. Hinged frames which are also removable are an advantage. For mosaics of this size, the Reverse method is the better one to use.

These mosaic units may be used on walls or for paving sections, but if a larger mural has to be done in this method, it is advisable to consult the contractors or builders as to the best type of wall fitting to be used, as this will be dependent on the wall surface. In some cases a hardboard backing is used for the mortar and this is fitted with heavy duty hangers at the back so that the mosaic may hang flat against the wall. The backing board *must* be waterproofed (see Waterproofing page 129) and the hangers fixed in before the mosaic is laid.

A thin layer of mortar is laid within the frames and a reinforcing wire mesh laid onto this before the actual setting bed is trowelled on. This technique is also described in example 1.

The method of glueing tesserae on to various types of backing board or prepared wall surface has become popular recently on account of the many new adhesives that have come on the market. New chemical combinations make it possible to find the perfect adhesive for every situation and condition and some of the *Unibond* and *Bondcrete* types are, as their trade name suggests, a strong bonding element for concrete. The tile cements and grouting cements which may be purchased in ready mixed packets are worth experimenting with, and for the more adventurous, some of the casting resins which may be poured over the laid-out mosaic will form a durable and impervious seal for the tesserae. At present they are rather expensive. They may be used for table tops or trays if you do not find their rather synthetic finish unpleasant, and are very widely used for these purposes in the United States of America.

After both these methods, as in the Reverse method, a final grouting is usually given, except in the case of the casting resin or when the material used is uneven and a rough natural surface is desirable.

An example of this method is given in chapter V of a mosaic made of ceramic tesserae set with *Unibond* adhesive, together with an illustration.

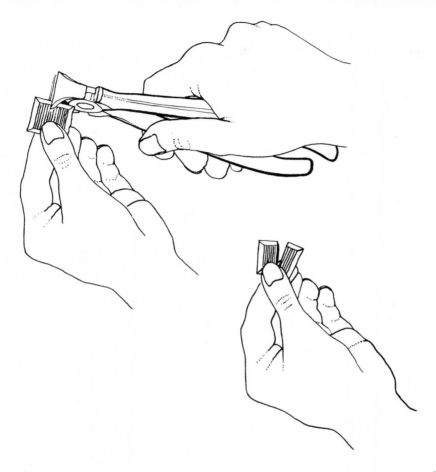

CUTTING TESSERAE

Vitreous tesserae, smalti, ceramics and tiles can all be cut with ordinary nippers, but the mosaic cutters illustrated (22) should be purchased if serious mosaic work is intended. They are adjustable to different thicknesses and produce a clean, accurate cut with a minimum of effort.

The tesserae should be held in the left hand at right angles to the cutter. With the tool held in the right hand, far up the handle, open the cutter edges and close them on to the tesserae about $\frac{1}{16}''$ to $\frac{1}{8}''$ over the side. With a sharp snip the tesserae should break into two as shown (22). Never place the tesserae right inside the cutter: it will be far more likely to shatter than to break cleanly as it will do if fractured on the extreme edge.

THE SEATED FIGURE

The first example of this technique is a decorative panel of 15″×30″ set in a cement mortar, done in three stages.

Materials (tesserae)

Smalti
Hand-made ceramics
Stained glass
Vitreous tesserae
Tiles
Mortar
1 part Portland cement
3 parts sand
1/4 part hydrated lime
1/8 part black cementone
Wood for framing
Softwood, 8′ length by 1″×1/2″
Chipboard backing (later removed) 15″×30″
Wire mesh, 1″×1/2″ gauge, size 13″×28″
Four clamps or weights
Plywood square, 1/2″×10″×10″ (for flattening tesserae)
Wooden batten for levelling

Tools

Glass cutter
Tile nipper or mosaic cutter
Small hammer
Wire clippers
Tailor's wheel (for tracing)
Mortar trowel

General carpentry tools for making frames

Method of working

After several preliminary sketch ideas, a design was decided on and a cartoon drawn out of a conventional type of seated figure of a scale matching the size of the panel. An important point to be remembered when designing a mosaic to fit into a given space is that the design must have the right relationship to the area.

A selection of mixed tesserae was chosen; smalti, ceramics, vitreous tesserae, tile and stained glass. The colours used were from a wide range of blues, from a dark royal to a pale eggshell, browns from deep peat to pale gold and amber, a greyish pink and a grey-white were included and where strong contrast was required, a small quantity of black.

The reverse side of some of the hand-made ceramics was used, giving the natural matt clay texture to set against the shimmering stained glass and smalti.

The main feature of this design was intended to be a contrasting pattern over smaller areas, giving an overall effect of a sampler, the tesserae being used flat in the main sections and sideways in parts such as the head where interest was to be focused.

Before the tesserae were laid on the cartoon, a second cartoon was traced out to lay later on the wet mortar.

A good supply of stained glass tesserae in various sizes was cut in readiness (see page 86 on glass cutting), but a glass cutter and some spare glass were kept in hand for cutting odd shapes as the work progressed. It was also necessary to cut the circular sections of the tiles, and the shapes for the feet. Most of the other tesserae were cut as required as the cartoon was laid out.

STEP 1

The cartoon was pinned to a drawing board which was angled slightly forward by slipping blocks behind it. The angle is for ease of work but must not be angled too steeply or the tesserae will slip down. They were tried out experimentally in several arrangements before the final plan was settled. As discussed in chapter I, this playing about with colours, different materials and placings, is an important feature in planning a mosaic.

STEP 2

The kind of tesserae, the colours and placings having been decided upon, they were now set along the lines and filled into the areas of the cartoon. It must be remembered that they must not be set closely touching each other, but a small space left between each one. The reason for this will become obvious when you start embedding them into the cement. The small amount of this which is displaced when the tesserae are pressed down, squeezes up between each one, and if no allowance is made for this it will soon be found that you have too many tesserae to fit into the frame.

In this design the tesserae were laid along the lines of the pattern rather than that of the contours as can be seen in the illustration (23) to stress the square unit motif of the sampler effect.

Regarding colour, the background was kept dark in tone by using mostly stained glass in black or a dark blue, and similar shades in vitreous tesserae, while the tones of the figure were in lighter blues and browns, the dark shades being used only when the checkerboard pattern was most in evidence.

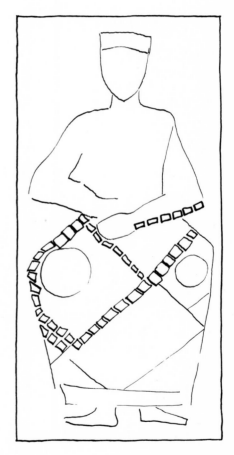

23 Tesserae laid on pattern line

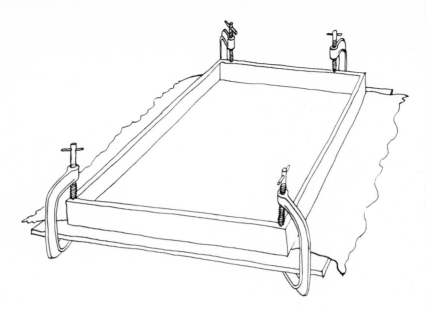

STEP 3

The laying out of the tesserae completed, the wood frame was made, (see Framing page 129) and laid onto the chipboard backing which was covered with a sheet of oiled lining paper (any form of vegetable oil or lard will do for this, and prevents the mortar from sticking). The type of backing board used is immaterial as it will be removed when the mortar has set, provided that clamps or weights can be fitted onto each corner. The frame was now clamped on to the board (24).

STEP 4

The wire mesh was cut to fit in the frame. It must be 1″ smaller all round than the framing and should be flattened as much as possible before it receives the

mortar. It was left in readiness beside the frame while the mortar was mixed.

STEP 5

The laid out mosaic and the frame ready for mortaring were placed as close together as possible for the transferring of the tesserae from one to the other. In this case two tables were placed parallel to each other and the artist sat on a stool between the two.

STEP 6

The first layer of mortar was mixed in the directed proportions, but no black *Cementone* was added to this mix. It was trowelled into the prepared frame, tamping down well round the edges and in the corners and finally drawing a wood batten across to level to a height of about $1/3″$.

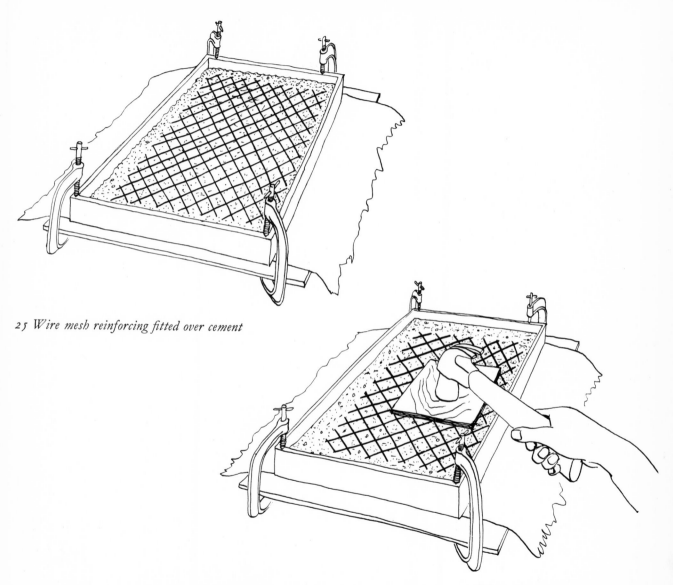

25 Wire mesh reinforcing fitted over cement

26 Wire mesh hammered into mortar

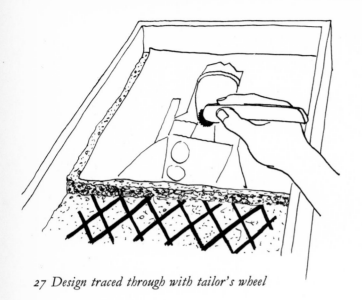

27 Design traced through with tailor's wheel

28 Mortar cut on pattern line

STEP 7

The wire mesh was laid over the bed of cement and pressed well down (25). The section of heavy plywood was placed over the top and hammered down firmly, to bed the wire mesh into place (26). Starting from the centre, it was moved all over the area of cement and hammered down in this manner. Then it was removed and the mortar left to dry for 24 hours.

STEP 8

The second mortar mix was prepared of a slightly less stiff consistency in sufficient quantity to cover one third down the frame. It is always advisable to prepare more mortar than you may need rather than to run short and have to make another mix.

STEP 9

The first layer of cement was thoroughly damped before the next mix was trowelled on to it. This, again, was well tamped down around the edges and at the corners, and after being brought up to the edges of the frame, it was again levelled off with the batten of wood.

STEP 10

The traced cartoon, which was divided into three sections, was laid over and the first section traced through onto the wet cement with the tailor's wheel. (The dampness of the cement usually moistens the paper sufficiently so that the wheel can cut through it and inscribe a clear line (27). The tracing was then removed and the traced line reinforced if necessary by incising it deeper with a sharp stick or a dental probe.

29 Edge of mortar

STEP 11

Transferring and embedding the tesserae now began, starting with the head section where it was important to be careful and precise. The tesserae were placed along the guide lines and gently but firmly pushed into place. Some of the larger ceramic ones, which were rather porous, had to be damped on the underside and then hammered down, care being taken not to damage the glaze. After a small area had been covered, the plywood square was placed on top and hammered all over to bed down uniformly. In some places where the tesserae were tilted or set sideways, this could not be done, of course;

if, however the cement is of the right consistency they should all press into place quite easily.

STEP 12

The ⅓ area was laid in just under two hours, by which time the cement was becoming appreciably harder. The final line of tesserae was not straight but followed the irregular line of the design (28). The remaining cement was cleaned off sharply at this point so that the next mix, which would be applied next day, would meet up against it as a vertical edge and not leave a thick line of cement between to show the join. Any surplus cement soiling the tesserae was wiped clean just before the mosaic was set (29).

STEP 13

A further mix was prepared and the work continued as described. Before laying and levelling the fresh mortar, however, the edge left from the previous day was thoroughly damped and this was repeated in the final stage of cementing.

STEP 14

The mosaic was left to set, uncovered in a cool workshop for five days, after which it was removed from the frame and the oiled paper peeled off the underside. It was cleaned again, this time using a stiff nail brush and a soft cloth. This completed the job (30).

STONES AND CERAMICS SET IN ADHESIVE (31)

The second example of the technique was done in pebbles and stones and ceramics, set in a bed of *Nic-o-Bond* plastic cement, which dries fairly slowly —2 to 4 hours—giving ample time to lay in the tesserae. The *Nic-o-Bond* was darkened by adding a small amount of black *Cementone*. The proportion was a square, framed in softwood and backed by 1/2" plywood.

It was designed in the random distribution method, by placing the various materials onto the wet mortar square and rearranging them until they composed themselves into a balanced pattern. The colours were all the muted tones found in ceramics, dull blues, greys, silver whites, set against the dark grey and cream pebbles, the matt surface of the stone contrasting rather dramatically with the gleam of the ceramic. The dark background helped with this setting.

31 Ceramic and pebble plaque

Materials

Pebbles and stones in grey, silver white and cream
Ceramics with various impressed surface patterns

Mortar

Nic-o-Bond Thikbed 1/2 pint tin
Black *Cementone,* a small part

Wood

Softwood, 4½' of 2" × 1/2"
Plywood, 12" × 12" × 1/2"

Tools

Mortar tools
Carpentry tools

Method of working

The technique for making this mosaic is extremely simple. The frame having been made and nailed on to the base plywood, a layer of the plastic cement *Nic-o-Bond* was trowelled on to a depth of 1". The stones and ceramics, having been placed in their final positions, were pushed into place. The stones which were set on edge on their sides, required to be bedded well down into the mortar, while the flatter ceramics were placed in more lightly and shallowly.

The mosaic was allowed three days to dry and left finally in its frame.

CERAMIC TILE MURAL BY GEOFFREY WICKHAM ARCA

This interesting work, which I have been allowed to reproduce here, could be termed a mosaic mural although the individual units are large in scale. It does, however, show the relationship that can exist between glass and ceramic tiles, both glazed and matt, and exemplifies some of the techniques discussed in this book.

The mural was designed for the entrance of an office building when approaching from the road beneath the building. It runs through the glazed walls and may be appreciated from both inside and out. Composed of tiles set in relief on a brick wall, it consists of about half black commercial floor tiles with white and translucent decoration fired on to them. The relief is further extended by deeper terracotta tiles, set out where necessary on brickwork that had been corbelled out for that purpose when the wall had been built.

The whole design was intended to read as a series of vertical panels, $27' \times 2' 3''$ on a wall of horizontally pointed bricks.

Materials

    Stained glass
    Slab glass
    Black commercial floor tiles
    Terracotta relief tiles
    Cement
    Sand

Method of working

Briefly the technique is as follows: A scale maquette was first made showing the forms, relief and colour intended, using the dark industrial tiles to act as a foil to the freely modelled relief tiles. These relief forms were of a size that could be fired (at 800°C) in a smallish kiln and the design was in part dictated by this requirement. If the illustration (32) is carefully studied, the sections composing the terracotta relief tiles can be clearly seen.

The black industrial tiles were decorated with underglaze colour and fired with a white tin glaze.

The stained glass was broken into small pieces and set in the correct position before firing. They were then fired a second time to fuse the glass in pools between the relief.

32 Sections of tiles joined to form unit

33 Setting in position

The completed tiles were delivered to the site where they were set onto the wall by a professional tiler (33) using the traditional mortar of 3 parts sand to 1 part cement.

See figs 34 and 35 for the final section and the completed mosaic.

Photographs of three further examples are given as they show in closer detail different methods of laying tesserae (36, 37, 38).

34 Final section

36 Head of a woman showing haphazard laying of tesserae

35 Completed mural by Geoffrey Wickham ARBS, ARCA

37 Head of queen showing haphazard laying of mixed tesserae

Head of a woman was carried out in vitreous tesserae with the exception of the necklace where golden smalti were used. The haphazard method of laying, combined with a dark coloured grout, gives a fairly lively texture to the conventionally designed head. The actual scale was three-quarters life size, so many of the tesserae could be used uncut while others were merely slit into rectangles or triangles (36). The mortar used was ciment fondu, 4 parts sand to 1 part fondu.

Head of a queen was made with four different types of tesserae. The top part of the background was almost entirely hand-made impressed ceramics in shades of turquoise green and blue, with a few stained glass tesserae in variations of the same shade. The crown was in mixed ceramic and the face in white highly glazed ceramic, placed at random, stained glass being used for the eyes, nose and mouth. The hair and body were in stained glass tesserae with a section of smalti around the base of the figure.

The cement used was *Fixtite,* a white adhesive that may be laid in small areas at a time. The white base allowed the stained glass to record its true colours. As may be seen from fig. 37 certain areas of the tesserae were laid on the contour lines while others were laid almost as loose chippings.

Abstract design (38)
This was carried out almost entirely in smalti, with only a few sections in impressed ceramics, all being laid along the contour lines of the design. It was set into *Fixtite* which was laid in small areas at a time, as in the head of the queen mosaic (37).

38 Abstract forms using contrasting material

The Indirect or Reverse Method IV

This method is so named as the traditional technique usually employed involves reversing the tesserae by first pasting them back to front on to paper and then turning the paper over and pressing it on to the wet cement. When the cement has set, the paper covering

the tesserae is damped and peeled off, revealing the completed mosaic with the tesserae now right side uppermost. Grouting is usually necessary to fill in the cracks and create a smooth finish and space must be allowed for this when laying the tesserae on to the cartoon.

The procedure is as follows: The design is first prepared and drawn out on to a squared cartoon (39) and a tracing is made of it. The tracing is always necessary where a large-scale project is contemplated.

The tesserae are now laid out experimentally on the cartoon (40) until a satisfactory colour and contour pattern have been arrived at. When this stage is completed and all the tesserae laid out, the tracing of the cartoon is placed beside it (41) and the transferring of the tesserae can begin. Each piece must be lifted out, spread with paste and placed on the tracing in exactly the same position, and the same way up as it was arranged on the cartoon (42). At this point it must be remembered that $1/12''$ space must be left between each tesserae for the grouting. The glue must now be left to dry for 24 hours.

The sections must now be separated (43); some will be squares and some must follow the contour lines as dictated by the design. In the Reverse method it is all too easy to become confused when setting

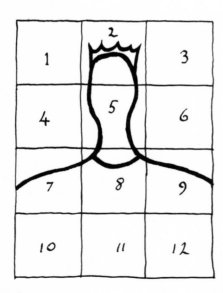

39 Squared cartoon

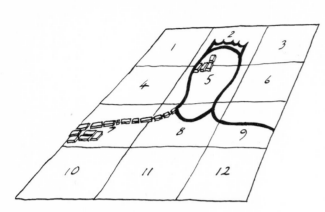

40 *Tesserae laid out experimentally*

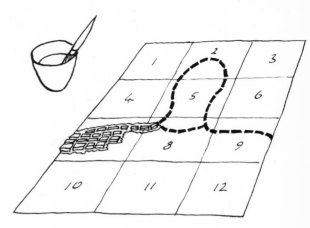

42 *Glueing down tesserae*

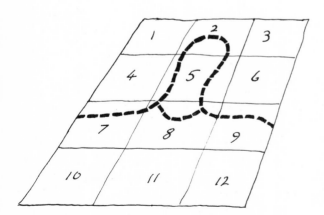

41 *Tracing of cartoon*

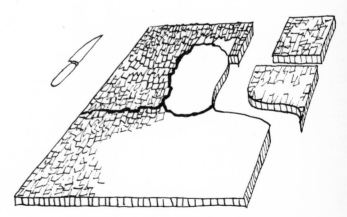

43 *Sections being separated*

these sections into the wet mortar, and it is helpful to prepare a numbered key, remembering particularly that the image will be reversed and the numbers will be the other way round.

The sections themselves are now numbered on the back and stacked for transportation (44).

44 Stacked, numbered sections

In the case of a large mural it is wise to have the wall prepared and the setting bed laid by a professional plasterer, as a vertical surface can present real problems if the cement is too wet and the mosaic sections slide down. Too much water can also cause the tesserae to become dislodged and drown in the setting bed. It is safer to lay an area of the setting bed for each section at a time (45), although if several assistants are available you can cover a larger area before the cement begins to harden. Some people prefer to work from the bottom upwards to avoid the sections slipping down and this is the best method if you are a beginner.

The tesserae sections are usually grouted before being laid on to the setting bed by being placed paper side down and a thin grout trowelled over them (46), filling in all the cracks, the surplus then being wiped off. (See recipe on page 128). The sections are then carefully placed in position on to the cement bed (47) paper side up, (noting as in the diagram the numbers now run from right to left) and pressed into the mortar. A flat board laid across and gently hammered is a good way of embedding the tesserae evenly.

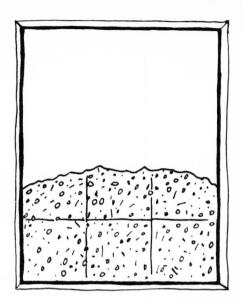

45 Section of cement setting bed

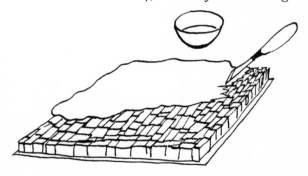

46 Grouting being laid over tesserae sections

The removal of the backing paper (48) must be done carefully when the cement is almost dry. If allowed to become too dry it will be impossible to make any small alterations or correct the position of tesserae that may have become misplaced. It will also be more difficult to remove the paper, which in any case must be thoroughly damped with a sponge before it is peeled off. If, on the other hand, the mortar is still too wet the tesserae will be displaced and the mosaic irreparably damaged.

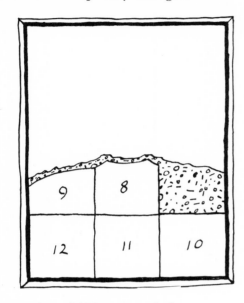

47 Sections being laid into cement bed

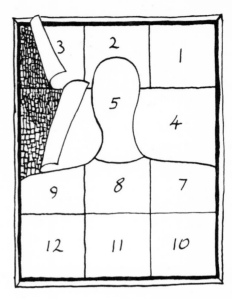

48 Removal of backing paper

The best thing to do is to test the set at one corner by peeling back a small section of the paper, preferably where the tesserae are placed as a background and do not form a part of the design.

Grouting may also be done after the whole mosaic is set in place and the cement hardened in the same way as described earlier. A wide rubber squeegee should be passed over the grout to level it and also to clean the surface. When all is completely dry and set, it must be thoroughly cleaned with a fine hard-bristled brush. A solution of muriatic acid can be used to remove any difficult cement deposits on the tesserae, but this should never be used on a coloured grout as it will bleach out the colour.

Several points should be noted in regard to this method. First its undoubted advantages. It is obviously the one to use when a completely smooth surface is required, as for a mural in a bathroom or kitchen, a floor or a table top—surfaces that need constant cleaning. Secondly, where a large-scale project is called for, the whole scheme can be worked out in advance and then transferred to the paper sections and taken to the site. This has the distinct advantage over the Direct method where the tesserae must be set in heavy cement units to be moved, or the artist must work slowly and laboriously on the mosaic *in situ*.

The Indirect method also has several distinct disadvantages. Using the traditional technique, only tesserae of equal thickness can be used, although it is just possible to combine smalti and commercial tesserae. Angling and tilting the tesserae, which give such lively reflective surfaces, is not possible and the final mosaic is inevitably more mechanical in appearance.

In the diagrams showing the stages of this technique the irregular separating of the sections is shown (43). This is to avoid a common problem that arises when the design is not a geometric one and the junction between the sections is often too clearly visible, spoiling the unity of the design. The cutting of the sections along the contour design and sometimes dog-toothing them (28, 29) avoids the obvious break where each division occurs.

It is also important to be sure that each section is bedded down to exactly the same level as its neighbour or the completed mosaic will become a landscape of hills and dales. The division of the mosaic into sections is unnecessary for a small-scale one of 1' square or under and it is obviously wiser to gain experience on one such as this before embarking on a large mural.

A COFFEE TABLE

This shows the practical application of mosaics for objects of everyday use and the choice of a coffee table seemed to have a fairly general appeal. The procedure is straightforward and the technique a slightly simplified version of the traditional one. For a beginner the best approach is to work out a mosaic design in geometric shapes before deciding on the final surface measurements of the table, the reason for this being that if a symmetrical pattern is decided upon, vitreous tesserae laid out according to the pattern and spaced correctly will give the final measurements. It must be remembered, however, that a certain latitude must be allowed or you may find parts of the tesserae overlapping at the edges, making the fitting of a finishing frame very difficult.

Materials

Vitreous tesserae in shades of muted pinks, greys, blues, whites and blacks.

Blockboard $18^1/2'' \times 37''$, $^3/4''$ thick
4 table legs, $15''$ high (any hobby shop or supplier)
Hardwood strip $^1/4'' \times 1^1/4'' \times 10'$ approx.
1 pint *Unibond* adhesive
Dunlop S 854 solution
Screws for table usually supplied with legs
Cement and fine sand (for grouting)
Strong tracing paper
Bradnails (for attaching frame)

Tools

Mosaic cutter
Hammer
Spatulas for grouting and spreading (these can be cut from cardboard)
Sponge or cloths
Mixing bowl

Method of designing

In the example illustrated it was decided to use a basically symmetrical pattern made up of squares and rectangles with a central motif of slightly more complicated design in which the tesserae would have to be cut and fitted. This resulted in a pattern which was very easy to lay out for a large part of the area and presented only a little more complicated work in the centre.

The colours used were variations on the shades of pinks, blues and greys, together with black and white, and these were moved about until the design took form. A good deal of black was to give a predominating feeling of contrast. The central star motif was kept intentionally loose in handling, as if it had been more precise the mosaic quality would have been lost.

Method of working

The method used here differed from the conventional one in that the tesserae were not laid down in reverse but right side up and the adhesive paper which was pressed on to them in sections was simply lifted up with the tesserae adhering and laid on to the *Unibond* bed and later peeled off. The procedure was as follows:

STEP 1

When the design was finally settled upon (49), with the tesserae lying *face upwards,* and properly spaced ($1/12''$ should be allowed for grouting) the area was carefully measured, allowing $1/4''$ extra all round.

49 Design laid out on hardboard

STEP 2

The blockboard was then cut to this final size—$18^{1}/_{2}'' \times 37''$—and the design squares marked on it (50).

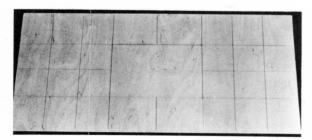

50 Table top marked out in rectangles

51 Table reversed, showing legs screwed on

STEP 3

The legs were then screwed on (51).

STEP 4

Tracing paper squares were now cut to a unit size of $12'' \times 9''$. This covered some six squares at a time, which was the largest area of tesserae that could be transported.

STEP 5

With a spatula, the tracing paper squares were coated with the rubber adhesive (*Dunlop* S 854 solution) which has the property of remaining tacky but retaining sufficient strength to lift the units of tesserae so that they could be removed to the table top. These squares were then laid on to the sections they related to and pressed down hard. Tracing paper was used so that the tesserae would at all times be visible through it (52) and any that had moved or fallen off could later be replaced. Small tabs of tracing paper not coated with adhesive were folded back to make a handle for easy lifting (53).

52 Tracing paper attached to central section for lifting

*54 Laying adhesive onto section before transferring
tesserae to it*

53 Lifting central section by holding tabs of tracing paper

55 Central section in place on table

STEP 6

With another spatula the table was coated with
several layers of *Unibond* adhesive up to between
$1/8''$ to $1/4''$ thick, coating one section at a time.

STEP 7

Each section of the tracing paper with the tesserae
attached was carefully placed in position on the
Unibond surface of the table (54, 55) taking great care
with the meeting of the junctions. The tesserae were
pressed well down with a flat board which was gently
hammered all over to ensure that they were all dead
level.

STEP 8

The completed table was turned upside down on the
floor and left overnight so that the *Unibond* would
grip properly.

STEP 9

The next morning the table was uprighted and the tracing paper gently peeled off (57). Any tesserae that had not held were replaced by hand using a dab of *Unibond* on the back.

STEP 10

A grout composed of 1 part cement to 3 parts fine sand with a little black *Cementone* added, was now mixed to a rather liquid consistency.

STEP 11

This grout was spread across the surface with a wide spatula, working well down between the cracks. In this instance two people worked, one spreading while the other wiped off the heavy layer of surplus grout (58).

56 All sections in place on table

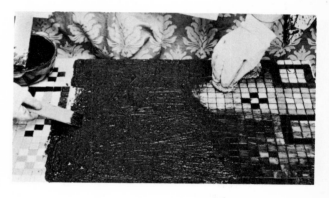

58 Grouting and cleaning

57 Removing tracing paper after tesserae have set

STEP 12

Finally the strips of wood were tacked to the edges of the blockboard with the bradnails.

STEP 13

A grout (this time mixed with a small quantity of *Unibond* to give adherence to the wood) was used to fill in the space between the tesserae and the edge of the wood and this was smoothed level with the surface with a small trowel (59).

60 *Table after grouting*

59 *Grouting edges between tesserae and frame*

61 *Finished table with edges painted black*

STEP 14

The whole surface was left to dry completely and then thoroughly cleaned and finally waxed and polished, and the edges of the wood painted black (60, 61).

A final point worth noting is that in a design of this nature, irregularity in spacing of the tesserae is generally an advantage in that it offsets the rather uniform nature of the design.

Completed owl of mosaic

AN OWL MOSAIC

The design for this was adapted from a photograph in a nature magazine. It was then squared out and enlarged (method described in chapter I) on to heavyweight tracing paper.

Materials

Venetian smalti
Commercial tesserae
1 lb plasticine
Plastic sheet ½ yard square
Open-mesh sacking about ½ yard square (clean)
2 to 3 ozs gum arabic
Metal mesh reinforcing (12″ × 12″ expanded metal ³/₈″ × ¹/₂″ mesh)
Clamps or weights (4)
Wood for framing 4′ 6″ × ³/₈″ × 1¹/₂″
Nails (2″)
Hydrated lime
Portland cement
Fine sand
Cementone (black)
Plywood baseboard (12″ × 12″ × ¹/₂″) waterproofed
Rolling pin or bottle

Tools

Mosaic clippers
Carpentry tools
Mortar tools
Wire cutters (for cutting reinforcing)
Tailor's wheel (for transferring design)
A wooden batten (for smoothing and levelling)

Method of working

STEP 1

The plasticine was first softened by warming slightly (modelling clay may be used for this operation instead of the plasticine and is considerably cheaper).

STEP 2

The plasticine was divided into four and rolled into balls.

STEP 3

These were rolled uniformly flat and then cut into square units of 4″ × 4″ approximately ¹/₂″ thick.

STEP 4

Nine of these squares were made and were then laid on the baseboard in rows of three to form the 12″ square required for the mosaic. The divisions were all pressed together with the thumb and the whole was rolled out to smooth and level it, thus slightly reducing the thickness. It was then measured and cut to an accurate 12″ square.

STEP 5

The traced cartoon was laid on to the plasticine and transferred by drawing the tailor's wheel along the design lines.

STEP 6

The tesserae which had been selected and set out in saucers were now laid on to the plasticine along the guide lines, when necessary clipping into shape to fit into place. As each section was completed, the tesserae were pressed down, setting the thicker ones deeper than the thinner ones, but never deeper than ¹/₃″ into the plasticine.

63 Retaining wall of plasticine

STEP 7

The tesserae were now all set into a satisfactory colour pattern, but several small alterations were made by shifting and replacing some with tweezers while others were straightened.

STEP 8

The entire surface was now flattened with a rolling pin or by placing a small plank of wood on top and gently hammering (62).

62 Rolling tesserae flat into plasticine

STEP 9

A strip of plasticine was rolled out and pressed round the whole mosaic in the form of a little wall so that the glue would be retained (63).

STEP 10

The square of sacking (previously washed and dried so that it was clean and porous) was placed over the mosaic.

STEP 11

The glue which had been prepared according to the recipe in chapter XI should be of thin syrupy consistency. If it is too thin, however, it will penetrate into the cracks between the tesserae and prevent the grout from entering, and if it is too thick it will not penetrate through the sacking. It was brushed generously all over the sacking surface and then dabbed into the fabric with a stiff paint brush (64).

Ordinary carpenter's glue can also be used for this job but the consistency has to be carefully judged. It also is applied hot. The glue has to be left to harden for 12 hours or until set.

64 Applying the glue

STEP 12

A board was placed on top of the mosaic and it was now gently reversed on to this. Working on the reverse side, the plasticine was gently peeled off and any tesserae that had failed to stick or had become misplaced were glued back again on to the sacking. The whole mosaic was now transportable and could, if necessary, be rolled up.

65 Plasticine being rolled off tesserae

STEP 13

In this case it was laid on to a square of oiled paper placed over the plywood and a test was made to ensure that the sacking was still flat. If it had warped or buckled up in any way it should be wetted with a fine sprayer until it is flat and even.

STEP 14

The prepared frame (see page 128) was placed round the mosaic and nailed in place on every side (66). If the frame is to be a permanent one, eight to twelve nails can be driven through the frame into the inside at regular intervals. These will bed themselves into the cement when it is poured on to the mosaic.

66 Framing and nailing in place

STEP 15

The expanded metal was cut to the correct size, half an inch smaller than the frame all round and tried for fit, making sure that it was perfectly flat (67).

67 Cutting wire

The following mortar was now mixed:

   1 part lime

   8 parts sand

   2 parts cement

It was mixed with water which was added gradually until it was of the consistency of thick syrup. This mortar was poured over the mosaic to a depth of ¼″ and pressed into the cracks with a stiff brush until they were completely filled with the grout mortar (68, 69 and 70). This was left to dry for an hour.

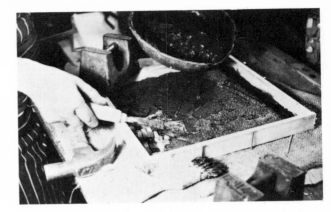

69 Stage 2

68 Grout being applied—stage 1

70 Grout being pressed into cracks with brush

STEP 17

The expanded metal was placed on to this grout mortar (71).

72 *Trowelling on mortar*

71 *Fitting wire reinforcing onto mosaic*

STEP 18

The following mortar was now mixed to fill the frame:

1 part cement
2 1/2 parts sand

Sufficient water was added to mix to a stiff consistency. Too much water will weaken the setting. This mortar was trowelled on evenly and tamped down until the water began to rise, special attention being paid to the edges near the frame and corners (72). A wooden batten was passed across the surface to give a level finish (73). Had the mosaic been intended to go on to a wall it would have been left rough and uneven to key it on to the wall surface.

73 *Passing wooden batten over to level*

STEP 19

After it had dried for three to four days (it is most important to ensure that it is absolutely dry) the nails were removed and it was turned over to strip off the sacking. This was stripped off gently, being easily removable as the dampness in the cement had caused the glue to become soft and gelatinous (74). If by any chance it should stick, sponge it with a damp sponge and it will peel off at once. Odd tesserae that may have slipped out of place should now be glued back into position with any handy adhesive.

74 Peeling off sacking

STEP 20

The wooden frame was removed by unhooking the hinged corner and lifting it away from the cement sides, taking care not to damage the edge by knocking it to free it from the frame.

STEP 21

The finished mosaic was laid sideways and sponged with warm water to remove all traces of glue and sacking (75).

A final example of the Reverse method is shown (76, 77). These two panels, each being 8' × 2', were carried out in the sectional method described at the beginning of the chapter and taken to the site in Ilford where they were laid on the prepared wall in one day by three people. The tesserae used were smalti and vitreous mosaics.

75 Final mosaic

76 Church mosaic panel 1

77 Church mosaic panel 2

Ceramic Tessarae V

Mosaics that may be designed from this type of tesserae range from great murals that cover the whole side of a building, the basic units of which may be of the maximum size that a kiln can take, down to small panels composed of minute tesserae that have been fired in a small test kiln. The size, thickness and shape can be of your own choosing, the colour alone depending on your skill with glaze mixing and firing. The texture treatment of the surface is an important part of the technique when one remembers that a mosaic of this kind is a shimmering face of perpetual movement, in changing light, alive and throbbing, and even on a large wall mural this quality must still emerge within the scale of the mosaic.

EQUIPMENT

A kiln – see Appendix for type and price (or the availability of a kiln)

Kiln furniture – consisting of batts to support shelves, props, shelves

A sieve – a 6″ diameter 120 mesh is usually sufficient

Seger cones – for measuring kiln temperature. Numbers O2a, O1a, 1a (78)

Scales – for measuring glazes. Postage scales are adequate

A rolling pin

Plastic measures

Plastic buckets

Brushes

78 Kiln props and cones

Cutting wire – for cutting clay
Palette knives, scrapers, pointed sticks
Scrim, heavy-weight plastic – on which to roll the clay
A plaster batt – for knocking up the clay. This can be bought or made from plaster of Paris (see page 128)
A pestle and mortar – is useful but not essential (79)
A flat tray – (similar to a developing tray) for melted wax
A metal ruler

79 Pestle and mortar

MATERIALS

Standard modelling clay – with a firing range of 1050° to 1100° C
Paraffin wax – 1 lb is sufficient (for coating the undersides of the tesserae)
Plaster of Paris – (if required)
Prepared transparent glaze – firing range 1050° to 1100° C)
Body stains – for using with slip
Glaze stains – to mix with transparent glaze to produce colour
Oxides – if you prefer to mix and blend your own colours. The following are usually required:
Iron oxide
Manganese oxide
Chrome oxide
Tin oxide
Black cobalt oxide
Black copper oxide, Copper carbonate
Flint or kiln wash – to coat the kiln shelves to prevent the tesserae from sticking
Ball clay – for making your own glazes
Lead bisicilicate (*Podmore's* P 29) – for making your own glazes

Other ingredients must be purchased if the more advanced glaze recipes are used.

These are the basic requirements for making your own tesserae, although other equipment and materials may become necessary as you progress. The collection of objects for impressing textures should be part of the equipment and your eyes should always be on the alert for these.

Standard modelling clay can be obtained from any pottery supplier in terracotta, buff or grey (see page 132), but if there is any opportunity to dig and prepare the local clay, the firing range would be a matter of experimentation. How to prepare newly dug clay is described on page 128. In Cambridge,

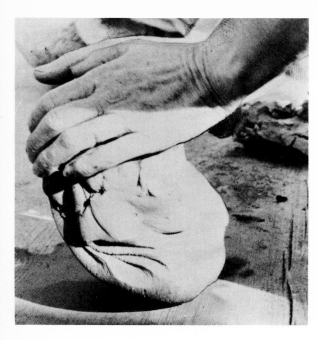

80 Knocking up clay—stage 1

the home of the author, the clay from Chatteris can be bought ready prepared and is widely used by potters.

Modelling clay from the supplier generally comes in hundredweight plastic bags and can be kept in these in a cool place or transferred to a reasonably airtight container and wetted occasionally if it shows signs of drying out. Never let the clay become quite dry or it will have to be slopped down (covered with enough water to saturate it) and dried out slowly until the right consistency is reached, a process that can take up to a week, depending upon the weather conditions. Incidentally, a separate bucket of water should always be kept to slop down any dried left-over clay so that it can later be used again.

The glazes should be transferred to glass screw-topped jars where possible and legibly labelled. The measures and containers should be kept very clean as a few grains of oxide left in the bottom can radically affect the next glaze that is prepared.

PREPARATION OF THE CLAY

This is begun by placing a good-sized ball of clay on a table or plaster batt (which may be obtained from suppliers or made from recipe in chapter XI), and knead it as you would for pastry. If the clay is rather too damp it is essential to have a plaster batt as this will absorb some of the surplus moisture. This knocking-up process, as it is known, expels the air bubbles that may be in the clay and makes it workable (80, 81, 82).

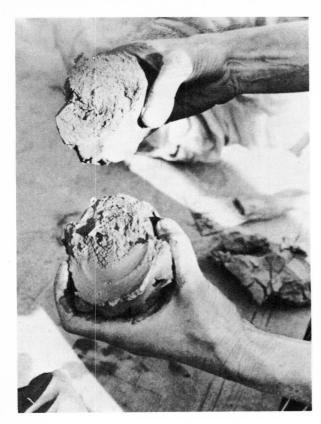

81 Stage 2

82 Stage 3

It is then placed on a square of sacking, scrim or heavy plastic, laid on a stout bench or table and rolled out with a wood roller until it reaches the required thickness; $1/8''$ to $1/4''$ is about right for tesserae. For accuracy, place a couple of wooden battens of the right thickness on each side and roll across these (83).

From this stage on there are two methods of treating the clay to prepare it to receive the surface treatments. In the first case it is allowed to dry completely, taking about a week. It is then given a light firing (900° C), known as the biscuit firing, and a glaze is applied following this. It is then re-fired at a higher temperature (1100° C), and although this method produces more intense colour, the second method is the one usually employed for tesserae making as it involves only one firing.

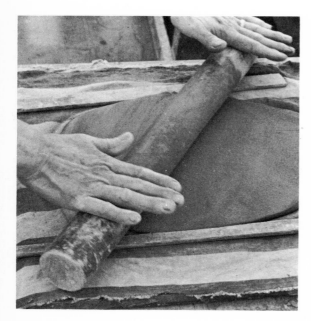

83 Rolling out clay

In this second case the clay is dried for a few hours only until 'leather dry', the surface treatments and/or the glaze is then applied and it is fired at the higher temperatures (1050° to 1100° C).

SURFACE TREATMENTS

Various forms of surface treatments are applied to the clay before glazing which enhance the reflective properties, giving greater vitality to the tesserae, are described below:

1 Impressing

This is done by stamping different pattern moulds on to the clay after it has been rolled out. The clay body must be of the right consistency to take this. If it is too soft and wet a sticky mess will result, and if it is too dry it will probably crack when pressure is applied. The illustrations (84, 85) show the various objects that can be used for this impress treatment, but you can also make little moulds yourself, biscuit-firing them. They are made as follows:

Roll up some balls of prepared clay of about the size of a small egg. Pinch together on one side to form a handle (86). Holding the mould by this handle, press it into some interesting surface (such as basket weave) to give a strong impression on the clay surface. When you have made a collection of these, put them in the kiln when a biscuit firing is being done. Many interesting impress moulds can be made in this way. Some suggestions of materials and things that you could press the clay into are: cogs and bolts, dried sticks, dried seed-pod sections, leaves, bark, the end sections of straw, cheese grater. Obviously original ideas will spring to mind (87).

84 Impressions from pinched moulds A

85 Impressions from pinched moulds B

86 Pinched moulds

87 Impressed tiles

2 Sgraffito

This is a very old technique which consists of scratching or scoring lines and patterns, either direct on to the leather-dry unfired clay or through a pigment, or on to the clay *after* the glaze has been applied. By scratching through the glaze covering with a sharp pointed instrument the raw clay beneath is exposed and forms a line pattern (89).

89 Sgraffito

88 Impressed textured tesserae

3 Wax resist

In this technique, the line pattern is drawn on to the almost dry clay with a wax pencil or sharpened candle end *before* the glaze is laid on. As the glaze cannot adhere to the wax, the areas covered by it are left clear of glaze, and thus form the pattern (90, 91).

90 Wax resist—stage 1

91 Stage 2

4 Flashing

For this treatment a very dilute glaze is used and wiped on to the clay lightly with a sponge, or brushed over with a large coarse brush before firing.

5 Pattern painting

Painting patterns on to tesserae is only worth while if you are making rather large-scale ones, two inches or more in area. The pigments used for this are simply prepared by mixing a teaspoonful of transparent glaze with a tablespoonful of water and adding very minute quantities of the required colour (suppliers' colours are suitable for this). This is painted over white glaze. Alternatively, underglaze colours can be painted direct on to a white slip and then glazed (92).

92 Pattern painting

6 Sanded texture (raised)

For red On to the raw clay brush a mixture of diluted clay (to the consistency of thin mud) and golden sand and fire this at 1100° C.

For white The same method as above but substitute silver sand for the golden sand.

OTHER TEXTURES

On to the raw clay many interesting shapes may be pressed by a slightly different method from Impressing. This technique needs fairly large tesserae to be at all effective, but would be very suitable for larger murals, possibly on outdoor sites. Some of the suggestions are: Twigs or branch forms, hay and corn grasses, fish backbones, sunflower or other large seeds, and, for smaller tesserae, try sawdust, wood-wool or smaller seeds. These are rolled or pressed into the clay and fired in the kiln in a reducing atmosphere. Under these conditions the pressed forms will burn away leaving only their imprinted pattern. Reducing should only be done under the guidance of an expert potter as it requires skill and experience.

SLIPS

A slip is a mixture of sieved clay diluted with water to the consistency of cream. The tesserae are either dipped into this mixture to coat their upper surface or this mixture is painted on. In both cases it is advisable to coat their undersides with wax before the slip is applied. Paraffin wax melted in an ordinary baking tin is used for this purpose.

Both slips and glazes can be coloured by the addition of oxides. A coloured slip can be covered with a different coloured glaze. An ordinary white slip gives a good base for any coloured glaze and can be used over a red or a grey clay if required.

GLAZES

A glaze is the glass-like coating that is applied to the clay body to protect it, to make it impervious to water and to decorate it. It can either be applied to the raw clay or after the biscuit firing, but, as mentioned earlier, is usually done to the raw clay in the case of ceramic tesserae.

In the process of firing both the clay and the glazes expand and contract, and because this expansion and contraction should measure the same in the clay as in the glaze, it is advisable to incorporate some of the clay in the glaze—up to 30% may be included.

Most pottery suppliers will, however, send a glaze to fit the clay they stock and it is only when a special glaze is required that the above rule of fitting the two must be observed.

The following glazes are recommended and can be obtained from Podmore and Son Ltd:
For use with:

CLAY	GLAZE
B 34/1 (1100° to 1150° C) buff	– W 165 transparent leadless – A 9 opaque tin (white)
B 31/1 (1100° to 1150° C) terracotta	– W 165 transparent leadless – A 9 opaque tin (white)

Of the two glazes mentioned above, No. W 165 is colourless and is added to the oxides or glaze stains in the proportion stated in the recipes. The opaque tin glaze No. A 9 has an attractive milky quality and when used in small quantities with the oxides or stains gives a semi-transparent sheen which is particularly suitable for tesserae. It is worth experimenting with.

APPLYING SLIPS AND GLAZES

Glazes are purchased finely ground ready for mixing and the usual recommendation is that sufficient water be added to give a finished pint weight of 31 per pint for all leadless glazes. Slips are mixed by adding water to the clay and stirring thoroughly. It should be of the consistency of cream—with water poured off if too thin or added if too thick.

Seed mosaic (see pages 111 to 114)

Both the slips and the glazes can be brushed on to the clay (93) and indeed for small quantities this is most practical, but it is always difficult to keep the buckets of solution constantly stirred, and the solid matter falls to the bottom leaving only a water mixture to be brushed on.

93 Brushing on glaze

The following is the better method where a slab of tesserae is to be dipped: Melt paraffin wax in a large baking tin (94) (of an area to take the clay slab) and dip the underside of the clay into this, coating it completely with wax. This ensures that no glaze melts on to the kiln shelf during the firing causing the slab to stick. When the wax has hardened, in a few moments, the clay can be dipped into the prepared slip or glaze, which must be kept well agitated. Again a baking tin or a large photographic developing tray is the best receptacle to use for this operation. Before dipping, be sure that the slab is free from dust or greasy finger marks, as this will prevent the glaze from sticking. Two coats can be applied but are seldom necessary if the right consistency is used.

94 Glaze trays

Do not attempt to dip too large a section of clay slab or it will bend and become warped or misshapen and the resulting tesserae will be difficult to bed down. Allow a short time for the glaze to dry before cutting into sections (95). It may be scored or cut into the required shapes before glazing or afterwards,

95 Cutting clay slab

although it is quicker to load a kiln with several slabs than many small tesserae. Do not confine your shapes to squares and rectangles; many other shapes and varied sizes should be prepared to build up a stock that will be used for many mosaics (96).

When they have not been separated before firing, they will come out of the kiln stuck together, but can easily be separated by tapping gently with a tack hammer on the underside or equally simply by parting on the scored line with a tile nipper (97).

FIRING

The kiln shelves (98, 99) must be coated with flint or a kiln wash before tesserae are stacked, even though the problem of running glazes should have been dealt with by waxing. Use 1½″ kiln props to support the shelves (78) one directly above the other. For tiles or heavy-weight tesserae, three props for each shelf are used, one at each back corner and one in the middle in front; this gives better distribution of weight and a little more room on the shelves. Four props are often used for light tesserae and should be placed before the tesserae are laid in.

For firing raw glaze, as in tesserae, although cones

96 Tesserae laid on kiln shelf for firing

97 Separating tesserae

98 Laying tesserae on kiln shelf

99 Stacking kiln

No O2a, O1a, 1a are placed in the kiln before switching on, the temperature must first be brought slowly to 750°C (as for biscuit). The spy hole bungs are then inserted and the temperature should rise to 1100°C. When the cones have bent to the base this temperature will have been reached, the firing taking anything from 9 to 12 hours depending on the size of the kiln. It is best to prepare the kiln the night before so that all will be ready to switch on early in the morning, and as firing is expensive, be sure and have a full load.

When the correct temperature has been reached switch off the kiln and allow to cool down overnight removing nothing from the shelves until the kiln is cold. The tesserae are then removed, separated, and stored in boxes or jars (never in tins).

It is always worth while doing several test tiles with each firing to try out different glaze experiments. Keep a notebook beside you with details as to quantities and variations in firing conditions for each group of tesserae made. If the colours are not what you expect (and they probably won't be the first time) you can vary the amounts of oxides or glaze stains very minutely, or try firing at a higher temperature. Infinitesimal quantities of oxides can give great variation in colour, and changes in firing temperatures may alter the texture, giving interesting crazed or run glazes.

Unlike pottery, where firing is nearly always fraught with anxiety, tesserae making always has a happy ending. Everything that is fired can be used for some mosaic or other—eventually!

GLAZES THAT CAN BE MIXED

The following is the basic recipe for a lead bisicilicate glaze which can be used with the colours below. It is approved by the Ministry of Education (non-poisonous) and is a shiny transparent glaze that fires at 1100° to 1160° C.

25% ball clay (*Chatteris*)
75% lead bisicilicate (*Podmore's* P 29)

Method of working

Weigh out the clay and the lead bisicilicate according to quantities. Have ready a bucket half full of water and put in the dry materials. Sieve through a 120 sieve, stirring before and during sieving. After this is done, allow to settle and if it is too thin, pour off excess water. Cover until ready to use.

FOR A SEMI-TRANSPARENT GLAZE
Add 5% tin oxide to the glaze recipe.
(If this is used over red clay (unslipped) the resulting shade will be a pale pink, but if it is fired above 1160° it will be a brownish grey).

FOR AN OPAQUE GLAZE (This is white and glossy)
Add 10% tin oxide to the basic recipe.

Glaze colourings

The following are some of the approximate shades obtainable.

To 100% of transparent glaze (*Podmore's* W 165) add the following:
Blue
$1/2$% cobalt
1% red iron oxide
1% copper carbonate
2% zinc

As a base for the above recipe a white slip should be used.
Green
To 100% transparent glaze add:
1–5% copper carbonate (or a bought glaze stain)

Red brown
To 100% transparent glaze add:
5–9% red iron oxide or try to dig local red clay. Slop this down with plenty of water and sieve through an 80 sieve. Or buy red clay from suppliers.

Yellow
First make a slip of 100% white ball clay and 5% red clay.
Cover this with a 100% transparent glaze to which has been added:
5% iron oxide (for rich amber) or
2% iron oxide
1% manganese (for a honey glaze)

Black
To 100% transparent glaze add:
1% cobalt
8% iron oxide
$2^1/2$% manganese

Silver
Paint black copper oxide on rather thickly to give silver tone.

Brown
To 100% transparent glaze add:
7% iron oxide
1% manganese oxide
Purple
To 100% transparent glaze add:
Manganese carbonate

The following is a section of rather more complicated glazes for those who have time and inclination for further experimenting. They fire at 1050° to 1080°C.

Glaze A (transparent)
    20 grammes lead bisicilicate
    70 grammes borax frit
    10 grammes china clay

Glaze B (transparent)
    91 grammes lead bisicilicate
    4 grammes zinc oxide
    5 grammes china clay

Glaze C (semi-opaque)
    80 grammes borax frit
    2.5 grammes zinc oxide
    12.5 grammes micronized sircon, grade 1
    5 grammes china clay

Glaze D (matt)
    36 grammes lead bisicilicate
    17 grammes borax frit
    4 grammes zinc oxide
    2 grammes tin oxide
    35 grammes waterground zircon
    4 grammes china clay
    2 grammes titanium dioxide

For each 100 grammes of these glazes, add the following oxides to obtain the approximate colours shown below:

Oxides	Glaze A	Glaze B	Glaze C	Glaze D
2 grms copper oxide	mazarin blue	medium blue	azure blue	sky blue
3 grms copper oxide	sea green	sea green	turquoise blue	turquoise blue

Oxides	Glaze A	Glaze B	Glaze C	Glaze D
10 grms iron oxide	treacle brown	treacle brown	chestnut brown	indian red
5 grms manganese oxide	mid brown	mid brown	purple brown	purple brown

Examples of ceramic mosaics are illustrated (100, 101).

CERAMIC (set with a direct adhesive)

This was another example of the random type of designing, using ceramic tiles and pottery tesserae. It was designed and set on the board in one and a half hours to show in an art school exhibition, the object being to display ceramics as a mosaic material.

Materials

Home-made ceramic tiles in varying sizes—3″ × 3″, 2″ × 2″, 2″ × 1″, 5″ × 3″ etc. Many surface patterns were stamped on them and while some had a high glaze, others were matt. Many muted tones were used.
Mortar
    1/2 pint tin *Unibond* adhesive
Wood
    6½′ × 2″ × 1/2″ softwood framing
    Chipboard baseboard cut to 14″ × 22″

Tools

    Spatula for applying adhesive
    Tile cutter
    Carpentry tools

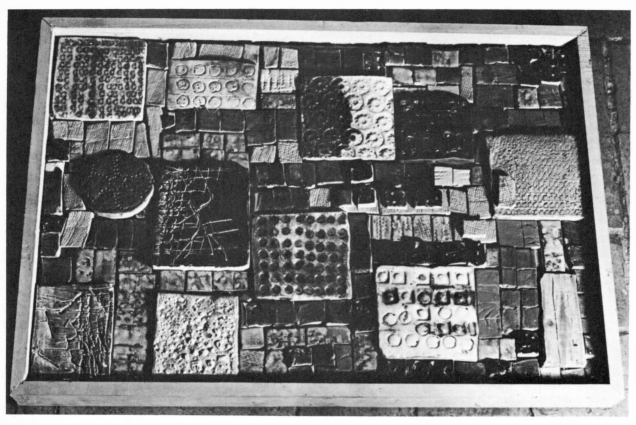

100 Ceramic mosaic

Method of working

The ceramic tiles, which were the result of various glaze tests over a period of several weeks, were all set within the frame and moved about until they formed a pleasing pattern of shape and colour. They were then lifted, one by one, and the adhesive brushed on the underside with the spatula.

The setting time was very rapid—a matter of ten minutes or so—and it was not possible to have second thoughts about the design.

No grouting was done to this or either of the two preceding examples as in all cases the spaces formed a part of the design. Fig. 101 shows an assemblage of ceramic materials combined with stones and mosaics.

101 *Ceramic assemblage*

Stained Glass Mosaics VI

By the use of stained glass as a mosaic medium some startlingly beautiful results are achieved. Several different technical methods are in use and it is very probable that others will be evolved by the creative and imaginative designer. Perspex also can be used in much the same way as glass, but with rather less interesting results as the colours are cruder and the material itself can never rival the glow and glitter of glass.

Several different kinds of glass are used for mosaics, depending on what you want to produce with it and the technique you employ. Cut stained glass tesserae are excellent for the conventional mosaic together with smalti and vitreous tesserae, provided they are used on a white plaster background or have been backed by gold or silver paint. If this is not done they will reveal little of their colour.

EQUIPMENT

Glass cutters (102) (single or multiple wheel)
Steel rule
Pliers
Cutter lubricant ($\frac{1}{2}$ paraffin to $\frac{1}{2}$ lubricating oil)
Palette knife (for puttying glass mosaic)
Graphite glass pencil
Glass cleaner
Polishing cloths
Felt pad or cloth (for cutting on)
Mortaring tools (see chapter II)
Hammer
Paint brush (for applying gold or silver backing)
Light box (103)

Stained glass (various types)
Plate glass
Slab glass
Bottle glass
Mortars
Adhesives
Putty mix (see chapter XI)
Backing boards
Reinforcing wire

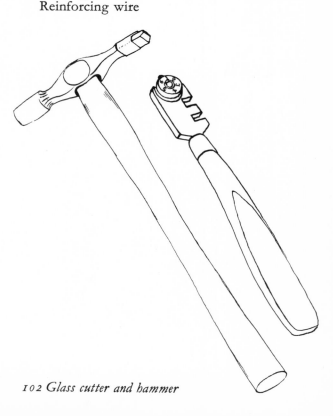

102 Glass cutter and hammer

84

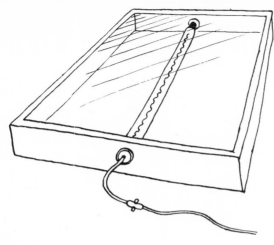

103 Diagram of light box

SLAB GLASS

This is generally obtained in sheets of 10″×8″ of an average thickness of 1″ (104). It is imported from France and although the price varies according to the colour, on the whole it is very expensive, especially the selenium shades of reds, yellows and oranges.

104 Slab glass cut and shelled

The technique of cutting this glass (105) is by no means easy in view of its thickness. It should be scored with a glass cutter in the usual way, dipping the cutter in lubricating oil first, and then tapped on the opposite side with a hammer (tungsten carbide tipped) until it breaks cleanly along the scored line. Some glass firms will cut cubes or rectangles of this glass if requested, but it is obviously worth mastering the cutting technique yourself. An alternative to cutting is 'shelling' and using the haphazard shapes with their facetted surfaces in a random design. Glass is shelled by tapping sharply up against the edges with the type of hammer illustrated in fig. 102.

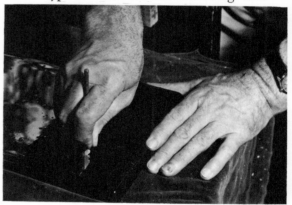

105 Cutting slabs

STAINED GLASS (traditional)

Several varieties of this are obtainable. It can be bought by the sheet, giving you the opportunity to choose the colour range you prefer and must be cut into the rectangular shapes required. The cost of it will vary considerably according to both the type of glass chosen and the colour. Ask to see the cheapest glass first as this is quite satisfactory for glass mosaics, always providing you can get the colours you want, but if more subtle shades are preferred, then you may have to buy better quality for a few of these colours.

85

Stained glass offcuts can often be bought and then you will not need to do any cutting. They should merely be sorted into colour groups and stored in boxes or similar flat containers.

Flashed glass should be mentioned as it has the colour fused on to one side only and as this side is much harder than the unfused side, cutting should never be attempted on the colour side. A brief cut will show you which side is which and this can also be seen when held sideways against the light.

BOTTLE GLASS

This can be collected both on beaches and at home. The glass from the beach is generally worn and sanded down by the action of the sea and can be used as it comes.

Ordinary bottles that have been collected, having lovely shades of deep greens and amber browns, must be broken carefully. Directions for doing this are given on page 32.

GLASS CUTTING

Clean the glass and lay the sheet of glass on a cloth or felt on a dead level surface and hold the cutter by one of the methods shown (106, 107). There is no right way to hold this tool provided it is held and maintained at right angles to the glass and it is better to experiment a little and find a grip that suits you best and seems natural. Find some odd bits of glass and practise the following method: lay a steel rule or metal straight-edge across the glass and draw the cutter sharply and firmly along it, applying slight but even pressure all the way along.

It must be emphasized that the glass should not be sawn by the cutter but lightly scored on the subsurface so that it will fracture on the drawn line. It is

useless to go over a line twice in an attempt to bite deeper as this will only bruise the glass and usually cause it to splinter across the area instead of down the scored line.

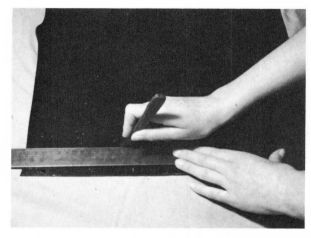

106 Cutting stained glass—method 1

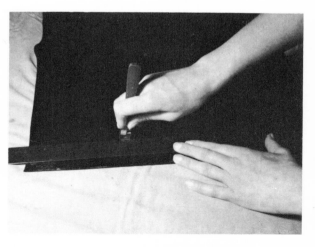

107 Cutting stained glass—method 2

Some prefer to cut towards themselves and others away from themselves. Whichever direction you prefer, try not to stop in the sweep of a cut, as each stop realigns the rotary wheels of the cutter, resulting in an irregular cut.

Remember to cut on the wrong side of flashed glass. Test by making a small score on each side.

For cutting practice for tesserae, score a sheet of glass in a series of parallel lines $3/4''$ apart, always cutting away or towards you, never across in front of you. Now turn the sheet round and score the other way to make $3/4''$ squares. You can, if you like, make rectangles or squares of other proportions. When you have scored the sheet (108) turn it over and gently tap across the lines with the ball end of the cutter. It will break easily into squares across the cuts. Remember that the glass is always tapped on the reverse side from the cuts.

108 Glass scored for tesserae cutting

Glass varies a great deal in toughness and one piece may be more difficult to cut than another. Hard glass can be laid along the line of the steel rule pressing the scored line against this edge or tapping with the cutter. Smaller sections which prove stubborn can usually be prised off with pliers.

Generally speaking, the more difficult shapes, such as circles, other curves and triangles, are not required for glass tesserae as these shapes can be built up from several small pieces, and the technique of cutting complicated forms comes within the province of the stained glass artist and is not for this book.

PREPARING GLASS TESSERAE

As previously stated, where stained glass is to be used in an ordinary mosaic (not as a translucent medium) it is necessary either to back it with some reflective material or to lay it on a background of white so that the colour will retain its brilliance. The only exception to this is when a black shiny tessera is required, as on an ordinary cement mortar almost any dark stained glass will read as black.

A light background can be created in several ways. Firstly, by any white adhesive used, although a plywood or hardboard ground will allow the colour to glow through. Secondly, a white setting ground such as plaster of Paris is equally effective, bearing in mind that this ground sets almost instantly and the Reverse method must be used.

Finally the tesserae can be used on a dark ground if they are backed by gold or silver leaf, copper or aluminium leaf which can generally be bought in booklets. It is not advisable to use ordinary gold or silver paint as the action of the cement may dissolve it, leaving the blank unreflective glass surface. Opinions vary about this however, and some artists say that the dissolving of the gold and silver paint can give a broken shimmering sheen which is unusual and interesting.

Gold and silver leaf being very thin (and very expensive) are difficult to apply, but aluminium achieves almost the same result and is probably the best to use.

Lay the uncut sheet of glass on the felt on the table, rough side up if textured, and brush the surface with waterglass. Lay the aluminium leaf together with its protective tissue on to the glass—a tricky operation that requires a delicate touch to do it accurately. Keep the windows and doors shut to avoid unnecessary draughts.

When the backing leaf has completely dried, the glass can be reversed on to the smooth side and you can begin cutting it. In applying the tesserae the leaf side is, of course, the one that is laid on to the mortar bed.

109 Marbles ready for firing

FUSING GLASS IN THE KILN

Both stained glass and bottle glass can be melted down in a kiln. Glass that has been fired and rendered smooth can be used as you would pebbles and stones, leaving them in the natural state that they leave the kiln. Or they may be cracked in smaller pieces from a flat fired pancake. The smooth glass shapes are ideal for children to work with and are the only form of glass tesserae recommended for schools and for small children. Marbles also may be melted down in this way, or used as themselves.

Break the sheet glass into the approximate sizes you want. If larger pieces are required it is better to put the pieces into a flowerpot saucer and it will fire as a pancake. In both cases the base of the kiln shelf or flowerpot saucer must first be coated with kiln wash so that the melting glass will not stick to the shelf. Ceramic grade whiting mixed with water can be used for this, having previously damped the porous shelves or saucer. Plaster of Paris or tin foil can be used also, but the latter has a tendency to amalgamate with the glass at higher temperatures.

Flashed glass is not advised for fusing, as it is very brittle and has to be fired at a higher temperature than other glass. It also loses colour.

Melting points

The following are the temperatures that must be reached to fuse glass.

GLASS MOSAICS

690°–730° C Thin glass begins to bend at edges.
730°–750° C Edges of stained glass are completely rounded.
830° C and beyond Further distortion takes place, glass begins to bubble and needlepoint. Heating beyond this point results in a molten state which may or may not crack when cool.

As has been seen, there are several ways of treating and preparing glass for use in mosaics and though the following examples show some different techniques for the use of glass, it must be remembered that it is a very effective medium mixed with other kindred tesserae such as smalti and ceramics.

EXAMPLE

Setting slab glass in concrete. It is a decorative method widely in use on the Continent of Europe and in the United States of America for both large and small-scale projects in domestic, industrial and church architecture. The example described is simply a small unit sample done to exemplify the technique.

Materials

The materials and their properties required for this work have already been described earlier in this chapter, but the approximate amounts used in this case are as follows:

2 half slabs, pre-cut into $1/2''$ cubes (mixed blues and ambers)

About half a slab of various sized chunks, cut as required or used from stock

Reinforcing wire (length $5' 6''$ fencing wire)

Mortar

1 part Portland Cement

$2 1/2$ parts sharp sand

Black *Cementone,* about 1 tablespoonful (for darkening mortar)

Water to mix (to which 2 tablespoonfuls of *Unibond* per pint was added)

Frame

This was made of $2'' \times 1''$ undressed softwood, and if it is to be removable, one corner should be hinged as described in chapter XI.

Method of working

STEP I

A sheet of heavy tracing paper was placed over the light box (110) (see description in Glossary) and the prepared frame laid over this. The designing which was carried out within this framework was done in the random method of placing the various coloured cubes of glass in different groupings, noting the shapes of the spaces left between as a part of the design. A few larger sections of glass were cut and some colours discarded and replaced until a pleasing pattern of shapes and colours began to appear within the frame (111).

110 Tracing paper over light box

111 Glass cubes laid on light box

STEP 2

The glass was now outlined with charcoal on to the tracing paper.

STEP 3

A second tracing paper which had been previously oiled on the back was placed on top of the glass and another tracing made. This was to serve as a key when the glass was surrounded and sometimes covered with cement.

STEP 4

The baseboard for the mortar was laid alongside the light box, the glass then transferred to it by the shapes being fitted back into their traced forms, one by one. At this stage it is still possible to make any small alterations that seem necessary. The first tracing was left on the light box for use later.

STEP 5

The wooden frame was fitted into place and clamped down at each corner. Weights can be used if the surface is a table top.

STEP 6

The mortar was mixed as described and of a rather stiff consistency.

STEP 7

The mortar was carefully trowelled in between the glass cubes, taking great care not to move any and continually tamping down and wedging the cement between each piece while holding it in position with a finger. Two people can do this job better than one. The whole area was covered to a depth of about half an inch to fix all the glass in position.

STEP 8

At this stage the reinforcing wire, which has been previously shaped to fit within the frame, was laid in position. It should fit half an inch in from the outside edge and be pushed down to bed into the first layer of mortar. It is shown in fig. 112 being measured for fit.

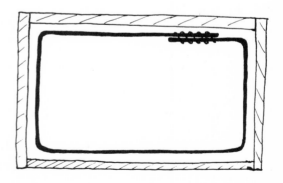

112 Wire reinforcing laid in frame

STEP 9

The second layer of mortar was applied, again wedging down around the glass and edges of the frame, especially at the corners. A flat-ended wooden stick is best for this job. Great care must be taken here to avoid the cement covering the edges of the glass from flowing over the top of it. If this happens it means the mix is too liquid. After this final application a check was taken by placing the second tracing over the whole frame and tapping through each traced outline to make sure that no glass cube was covered. In trying to get this layer level it is quite possible to cover a low-lying island of glass.

STEP 10

It was now cleaned carefully and a cloth laid over the whole mosaic and it was left to dry. It should not be damped as this is liable to draw salts out of the cement and cause blooming. After about four days cement should be set and the mosaic may be removed from the frame by gently tapping the wood round the edges and lifting out.

This type of mosaic can be used framed suitably and set on a stand when it can be placed against a window to show the full richness of its colour. Or it may be set on a table or shelf against a dark background and artificially lit from behind, where it will glow and scintillate brilliantly.

Large-scale mosaic murals can be used as room dividers or as screens. These should be constructed by planning in manageable units that will later be fitted together in a suitable framework, and for most purposes these units should not exceed 2′ × 2′ square. Beyond this size they are impractical to work on and are difficult to move. It is essential that they have wire reinforcing around the edges set into the mortar to help the weight of cement and glass that must be contained.

An example of this type of unit mosaic mural is shown (113). The basic units were 24″ × 20″. Three of these were slotted on top of each other within a framework giving an overall mural of eight windows six feet high. These were done for a small modern church in Kent. A further example in slab glass which has been shelled is shown (114).

113 St Mary Cray glass mosaic

114 Example of shelled glass panel

GLASS ON GLASS TRANSLUCENT MOSAIC

The materials and equipment needed for this type of work have already been mentioned earlier in the chapter, but the special requirements for this were:

A selection of cut glass tesserae approximately ³/₄″ square. Colours: bottle green, golden brown, lime yellow, deeper yellow, pale lilac, deep purple prussian blue and a pale aquamarine

Backing glass   A sheet of 32 oz (glass size)

Clear *Bostik* adhesive

Method of working

STEP 1

The design idea came from the cut section of an agate, much enlarged. It was first drawn out on a sketching pad into a satisfactory form and then translated on to heavy tracing paper with a felt marking pen to give a strong legible line contour. This was done free-hand, but the enlargement could be done by the squaring method as described in chapter I.

STEP 2

The sheet of glass was now cleaned and polished with a soft cloth. The cartoon was laid over the frosted glass light box and the sheet of glass on top of it (115).

STEP 3

The light box was illuminated and the colour selection made by viewing over the light. Have the light box placed in the darkest part and not before a window if you wish to gain fullest advantage of it. Various sheets of different coloured glass were held above until a good colour combination was selected.

115 Traced design over light box

STEP 4

Quantities of the tesserae were now cut and heaps of the various colours were laid in groups near the design on the light box.

STEP 5

The cut tesserae were laid along the contour lines of the design. As a general rule the lighter shades were placed against the darkest ones and the intermediate ones fitted in between to emphasize the contrasting lines of the agate form. They were laid on the glass in sections and as each section was completed, the glass was glued down with *Bostik*. An alternative to this method is to lay down all the tesserae, completing the whole design before glueing any down. In certain places the tesserae were laid one on top of another and glued two or three deep to enhance the depth of colour (116).

tesserae. It can be pressed in with the fingers, which is still the best method although the most hazardous, as it is almost impossible to avoid cuts. Alternatively it can be forced in with a rubber squeegee, which takes longer but is generally less painful. When all the cracks have been filled in with the putty, the glass is cleaned with crumpled balls of newspaper, worked well across all the surfaces until the glass is clear of any black putty. It must be cleaned again the following day. This dark putty gives a very beautiful stained glass quality to the mosaic and is well worth the extra trouble.

116 Translucent glass mosaic

STEP 6

The whole design being completed, it was left to dry for 24 hours and then the glass was cleaned with a soft rag dipped in turpentine. It was now suitably framed or put *in situ* as required.

A variation on this technique is to putty between the tesserae using the recipe in chapter XI. This putty is worked into every crack and join between the

GLASS FILAMENT MOSAIC BY TOM FAIRS ARCA

This is a most interesting mosaic using off-cuts of glass in the form of thin filaments which may not be readily obtainable but can sometimes be picked up from the larger glass suppliers or cut by yourself.

The design was limited to the end result; a fine linear texture and the effect aimed at was a richly coloured, closely textured area.

Materials

Stained glass filaments—usually pale tint colours because using them on edge tended to strengthen their colour. Ordinary pot metal colours would read as black.

A sheet of plate glass for the background
Cement – *Araldite*
Grouting cement – (Casting resin can be used if a transparent background is required)

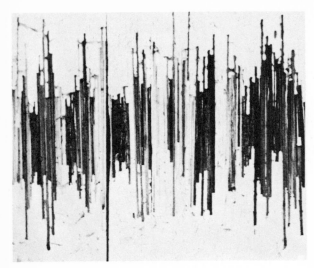

117 Glass filament mosaic 1 by Tom Fairs ARCA

Method of working

The stained glass is prepared, if necessary by cutting into filaments about 3/4" wide by various lengths.

STEP 1

The cut filaments were placed in bundles packed together like playing cards and cemented together with *Araldite,* having previously been arranged on the background sheet of glass according to the design.

STEP 2

When the bundles had been disposed satisfactorily they were cemented on to the background sheet, again using *Araldite.*

STEP 3

Grouting was now carried out with a fairly thin cement. In the final result the light is transmitted through the glass seen edge on. The depth of colour can be influenced to a certain extent by varying the

118 Glass mosaic by Anne Hodson

thickness of the individual filaments. If the light falls on the surface of the glass (i.e. no light transmitted through it) the effect is a sculptural one. In this case the glass mosaic was to be used as a decorative panel, but where a mosaic of this type is to be used as a room divider the design must be made on two separate sheets of lighter weight glass and then cemented back to back so that the design articulates (117).

This would be a most suitable type of glass mosaic to use as a room divider, a shower screen or simply as a decorative panel against a window or in place of a window.

Figs 118, 119 show examples by Anne Hodson.

119 Glass mosaic by Anne Hodson

Pebbles, Stones, Flints and Fossils VII

Several examples of pavements and wall treatments using a variety of stones and pebbles are given in this chapter, and it is hoped that they may serve to stimulate ideas of arrangements and uses of these fascinating materials.

While it has been possible only to give a general picture of the specimens obtainable around the coastline of England and in a few of the quarries, a far richer field exists in America and in some of the mountainous regions of Europe and the U.S.S.R. Idar Oberstein in Germany is a source of wonderful quartzes and agates, and pebbles polished by glacial streams can be found by rivers in Switzerland. The searching out and collecting of interesting minerals such as these can turn an interesting holiday into an exciting quest.

Flint is one of the commonest and most decorative stones found in England, but unfortunately the pattern and colour is only revealed by splitting and this is a job for an expert. It is an ancient craft that is fast dying out, but the practice of flint-knapping is still carried out in some rural areas such as Grimes Graves, at Brandon in Norfolk, where it is sometimes possible to buy off-cuts for pavements and walls. The photographs (120, 121) show a pavement made from a wide variety of flints found at Grimes Graves.

Stones and pebbles need no preparation beyond cleaning. In the United States of America, where tumbling machines are readily available, they are often polished, and the brilliant glass-like surface thus obtained brings hidden colours alive. The dullest pebble becomes a glowing jewel. Unfortunately, tumbling machines are rare in Britain and having stones polished professionally is exorbitantly expensive, so where great quantities are needed, polishing is out of the question. It is possible to polish pebbles by hand—some respond better than others, depending on the hardness and quality of the mineral, but on the whole it is a very laborious process and only recommended for amusement. Often a group of children will be entertained by sanding and polishing, and even a few pebbles thus enhanced will improve an otherwise dull mosaic (122).

For polishing by hand, buy several grades of the type of emery paper known as wet-dry—a medium to coarse, a medium, and a fine grade are adequate. The pebble to be polished is dipped in water every few moments, never allowed to become quite dry. Start with the coarsest grade emery and work through to the very fine for the final polishing, remembering that for a mosaic it is only necessary to polish one side of the stone.

An easier but less pleasant looking alternative is to varnish the pebbles with one of the clear varnishes, again only the part that will project above the mortar.

120 View of flint pavement

121 Detail of flint pavement

122 Polished pebbles

OUTDOOR USE OF PEBBLES

Since the earliest of times, in every corner of the globe where stones and pebbles have been plentiful they have been used to make patterns on streets, floors, courtyards and walls. Different peoples in such widely differing places as China, Spain, Mexico, Rome and Ancient Greece have used this enduring and beautiful medium to cover the ground and the sides of their buildings. It seems strange that they are not more widely used today, until one considers the amount of labour in man-hours.

To lay your own pavement, working slowly over a period of time, is still a possibility however, and several examples of this work are shown in this chapter.

There are two basic methods of working. The first one is to make a series of pebble inlaid concrete blocks. They can be round, square or indeed any shape you wish.

The second method is to lay the pebbles direct into the wet mortar bed *in situ,* separating the areas by paving stones, tiles, prefabricated concrete blocks or bricks.

Method 1

STEP 1

The shape is decided upon and a framework made, in wood if it is to be removable or in strip metal if it is to remain as a retaining wall.

STEP 2

The frame is placed on a plywood board and held in place with nails around the outside.

STEP 3

An area of reinforcing wire mesh is cut to fit within half an inch of the edge of the frame.

STEP 4

Make a mortar of 1 part cement to 3 parts sand, adding to each pint of water used 2 tablespoonfuls of *Unibond* to ensure that the pebbles stick.

STEP 5

Level this with a flat stick and mark out design decided upon with a sharp stick or a tailor's wheel. The mortar must be firm and fairly stiff.

The pebbles should now be laid in, keeping to the design marked out and working from the centre outwards. Leave for several days to set properly. (See fig. 123).

123 Pebble pavement unit

Small pebble inlaid tiles or plaques may be made in this way by using cake tins or small baking tins which have been well greased to prevent the mortar from sticking. It is possible to build up a supply of pebble plaques over the winter months, working indoors, and lay them in their patterned form into the wet mortar bed in the summer months to make a pavement. Several points must be observed when laying in the pebbles in a design. The areas should be grouped with pebbles which have a unified shape, size and colour to give contrast and form to the pattern. They can be angled, laid flat, or laid on edge, provided they are well bedded down into the mortar by hammering them two-thirds into the mortar.

They should always be grouped fairly close together; if you do not have enough to do this, it is better to leave areas of mortar than to have areas of sparsely patterned stones.

Method 2

STEP 1

The side should be measured and pegged out with a line of string to surround.

STEP 2

When the site has been levelled, a layer of aggregate is laid ($1/2$ gravel) and spread with a mortar of 4 parts gravel ($1/2''$) 4 parts sand and 1 part cement.

STEP 3

The paving slabs, bricks, or whatever you intend to use, should now be laid, working on a small area at a time.

STEP 4

A mortar mix of 3 parts sand to 1 part of cement is now prepared and trowelled into the spaces between the other units.

STEP 5

The selected pebbles are set in whatever formation has been decided upon into this mortar and bedded down by pressing a board over the top and hammering down.

This completes a section of the pavement, and further areas may be laid by the same method when the first part has set. On commencing each new section, remember to wet the hardened mortar thoroughly before trowelling in the new lot.

Many variations are possible within these methods, and the same treatment can be applied to any surfaces—walls, the base of pools, or interior situations.

TYPES OF PEBBLES

The following list gives the types of pebbles, rocks and stones, classified into locality, colour, etc., that may be found around the coast of England. It is possible in a book such as this to give only a very general idea of what can be found and all the interesting minerals from quarries have had to be omitted. If, however, you become interested in pebble mosaics to any extent, there are geological publications specialising in minerals, pebbles and fossils and these interesting magazines are often available at public libraries. Geology departments of museums can be very helpful, and of course the Geology Museum at South Kensington in London is a fascinating and informative place.

The collection should always be stored in wood or glass containers as tin can cause bad discolouration by rust. Large kitchen storage jars or square acid jars are ideal and make a decorative feature in themselves when filled with pebbles and covered with water to keep alive the natural wet colour of the stones.

Reds

Serpentine	(ovoid) The Lizard, Cornwall
Agate	(banded) Cromer, Aldeburgh, Felixstowe, Ramsgate
Carnelian	(translucent, horny, but often worn ovoid) Cornwall, Kent, Suffolk (Felixstowe), Norfolk (Cromer)
Jasper	(sometimes striped) most beaches
Sandstone	(ovoid) Norfolk, Kent, Dorset, Devon
Red slate	(fissile, lustrous, sometimes slightly crystalline) Devon, Cornwall, Wales

Browns

Jasper	most beaches
Chocolate stone	Harwich
Carnelian	(translucent) as for reds
Dolerite	(ovoid) East Coast, S W Coast
Chert	(angular, sometimes rounded) Kent, Dorset

Greys

Flint	(irregular) most beaches
Chalcedony	(fairly rare) Perthshire, Norfolk, Suffolk
Dolerite	as for browns
Schist	(fissile, shimmering lustre, flattened ovoid) North Wales
Onyx	(clouded) fairly rare
Chert	(irregular) Kent, Dorset
Granite	(rounded) Dartmoor, Cumberland, Cornwall, Scottish Highlands

Blacks

Jet	(lustrous gloss, irregular) Whitby, Felixstowe
Chert	(irregular) as for greys
Basalt	(irregular) Isle of Staffa, N. Ireland, many beaches

Oranges

Carnelian	as for reds
Smoky quartz	(crystalline) Cairngorms, Scotland

Blues

Blue shale	(ovoid, round) Chesil Bank, many other beaches
Blue slate	(fissile) Ilfracombe, other beaches
Dolerite	Grey-blue, many beaches

Greens

Schist	as for greys, North Wales

Serpentine	(ovoid) Cornwall, Anglesey
Jasper	as for reds
Greenstone	Cornwall

Yellows

Serpentine	as for reds
Carnelian	as for reds
Sandstone	Norfolk, Kent, Dorset, Devon
Smoky quartz	Cairngorms, Scotland
Citrine	(round, ovoid) Cornwall

Purples

Amethystine	(crystalline) Cornwall
Slate	as for reds
Jasper	as for reds

Pinks

Rose quartz	(crystalline) Cornwall
Agate	Norfolk, Suffolk, Kent
Sandstone	most beaches

Whites

Opaque quartz	Cornwall
Flint	most beaches
Chert	as for greys

MISCELLANEOUS

Ammonite Fossils

The Spiral Fossil, or Snakestone. These are generally dark grey but can be found in other shades, according to whether they are bedded in cliffs of limestone, chalk, shale or sandstone. Some are intermingled with crystals and others are covered with iron pyrites (fool's gold) and shimmer with a brassy lustre. They are more common than is supposed and can be found in quantities at Lyme Regis in the subsiding cliffs of blue lias, also in the East Cliff at Whitby, Hunstanton in Norfolk, Folkestone and quite a few beaches where the cliffs are limestone, shale or chalk. They are also abundant in many of the inland quarries such as those along Wenlock Ridge in Shropshire.

Pudding stone

This is a Conglomerate, a stone composed of tiny pebbles cemented together by some substance like silica. It is often very decorative when found in a dark shale pebbles of white quartz scattered over the surface. Braccia is a similar stone but the fragments are usually more rounded. These are found at Torquay, but pudding stones of many varieties are found on most beaches.

Iron pyrites

This has already been mentioned as a brassy covering to ammonites and other fossils. In crystalline form it is an opaque metallic yellow, but is more commonly found as veining through another stone or on slate or coal. It abounds in Penrhyn slate quarries, North Wales, but can be seen in Cornwall, Dorset and on other coasts.

Mother of pearl

This covering can be found on ammonites at Folkestone in Kent, and is another very decorative surface.

Marble

This is obtainable from many quarries, but is more easily bought as chippings from monumental masons. White and other stone chippings can be also be found here.

Several examples follow of projects carried out in pebbles, stones and flints.

PEBBLE-FACED MANTELPIECE
(124, 125) BY JOHN HAWARD

Materials

Stones and pebbles from the Cromer Ridge, Norfolk.
Mortar
   1 part cement
   1 part lime
   4 parts sand

Method of designing

A free design of geometric origin adapted to fit in
with the shapes and sizes of stones available.

Site

The mantelpiece panels of a fireplace in a Norfolk
flint cottage.

124 Detail of pebble mantelpiece surround

Method of working

When sufficient stones had been collected—white,
grey and reddish browns were used—a wood frame
was placed round the area to be cemented and the
mortar mix trowelled on. This mix was fairly dry,
but not too dry to inbed the stones. The outline
of the design was lightly scored into the mortar and
then the stones were laid in, being gently hammered
into place.

   The three different motifs of the design could be
done in three stages with different cement mixes, if
sufficient stones could not be collected for the whole
panel. In this case the edge of the finished panel
should be thoroughly damped before the new mix
was laid against it.

PEBBLE PAVEMENT MADE WITH PREFABRICATED MOULDS

This pavement was designed and carried out by people who have a cottage on the Norfolk coast, across the marshes from which lies a great shingle bank, famous for its stones and pebbles. As both the family and visitors had already made an interesting collection of these, it was decided to make them into a pavement which would thus provide a permanent situation for them.

The work was done mainly at the weekends and more pebbles were collected as required, as a very large selection is needed for a scheme of this kind.

The pavement was situated on a rectangle on the south-east side of the cottage.

Materials

Stones and pebbles from Salthouse beach, 2″ diameter approx. oval
Mortar
  Sand, cement, hydrated lime

Tools

Ordinary mortar tools

Method of designing

This was worked out from a tile pattern in the Alhambra (Spain) and adapted to size for use as a pavement unit (126). The thickness of the moulds was based on the thickness of a brick.

126 Alhambra tile design

Method of working

When the size, colour and shape of the pebble had been decided upon they were sorted into groups and piled in heaps on a long trestle table placed near the pavement construction. Although in this case many shades of pebbles were used, some may prefer to work in more contrast and use only black and white between the concrete moulds.

Construction of the concrete moulds

A template was cut in thick paper to the measurements as shown in the diagram (127). This was taken to a local carpenter who cut six moulds to the specifications in 2¹/₂″ wood. A heavy wood tray was used as a baseboard, the wood moulds were placed on this and screwed down firmly by means of the wood and metal frame as shown (129) and the following mortar was pressed between the moulds:

  3 parts sand
  1 part cement

mixed dry, adding only sufficient water to bring it to a crumbly state. The approximate quantity needed for the two blocks was measured into a bucket using a small coal shovel as the measure. 6 heaped shovels of sand to 2 of cement were required.

This mixture was packed well down between the wood moulds as shown (139, 131), and then rammed closely in with a hammer, paying special attention to the edges. The moulds and the attaching frame were now removed and the concrete moulds on their base board taken to a cool place to set, this taking about 48 hours. They were covered with a damp cloth throughout. Note: although the quantity given here is sufficient for the making of two moulds, four or more can obviously be made if sufficient mortar is mixed and other baseboards available.

Preparation for laying the pavement

The site was measured and then prepared by levelling and rolling to a firm level base. A thin layer of ¹/₂″ gravel aggregate was laid on before the foundation mortar was spread, using the following mix:

  1 part cement
  4 parts sand
  4 parts ¹/₂″ gravel

This was levelled by drawing a board over and checking with a spirit level. After this the following

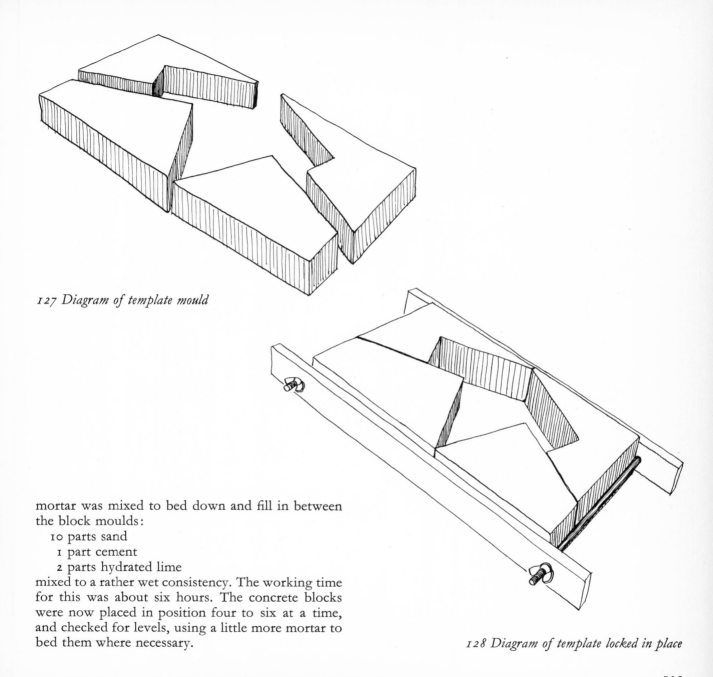

127 Diagram of template mould

mortar was mixed to bed down and fill in between the block moulds:

10 parts sand
1 part cement
2 parts hydrated lime

mixed to a rather wet consistency. The working time for this was about six hours. The concrete blocks were now placed in position four to six at a time, and checked for levels, using a little more mortar to bed them where necessary.

128 Diagram of template locked in place

129 Frame and moulds

130 Frame being fitted round moulds

131 Cement packed between template mould

the right amount of mortar (depending on the wetness of the mix) so that the pebbles are embedded to roughly half their depth. They were laid according to their pattern as shown (132). Each one was gently hammered down as it was laid, bringing them all as nearly as possible to the same depth and finally as each unit was completed a board was passed over, as before, and pressed down. Any pebbles that persisted in projecting too high were hammered down again until the board could rest on a level with all the concrete blocks.

The area that was finished was left to dry normally, although in very dry conditions a sack could be laid over.

By this method a fairly large section was completed each weekend (133). Fig. 134 shows another example of a pavement laid in small bricks in a herring bone pattern.

The spaces between the moulds were filled up with this mortar, using sufficient to bring them to almost the same level as the blocks, before ramming it well down. A little practice is needed in judging

132 Pattern laying

134 Pavement in small bricks in herringbone pattern

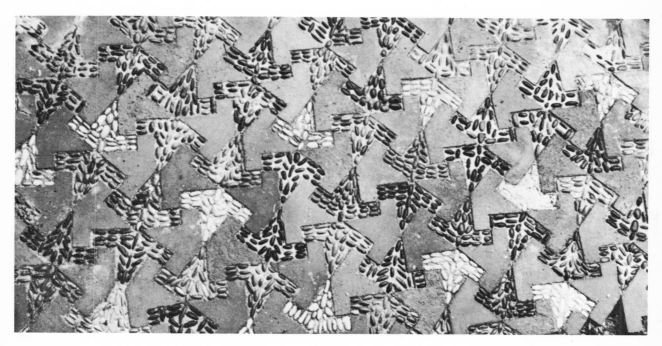

133 Completed pavement

Seed and Bark Mosaics   VIII

The range of materials for this type of work is quite wide and while it is possible to use very small seeds such as mustard, rice, lentils, wheat, pearl barley, etc., remember these will either have to be handled with tweezers or sprinkled on to glued areas and then pressed down. A fine variety of material may be found among the larger beans, butter beans, haricot, broad beans, coffee beans, dried peas and the many dried beans in varying colours to be found in the continental delicatessen, especially in Soho, London, or at any seed merchant.

The garden and countryside provide many interesting seed heads such as poppies, lilies, tulips, giant cow parsley, peonies, irises, and of course the countless seed forms from trees, acorns, sycamores, to mention only a couple. Seeds from vegetables and fruit should not be forgotten, pumpkin and marrow, melon, orange and lemon pips.

If this type of nature mosaic interests you, like the stone and pebble ones, it can give purpose and interest to country walks and to autumn days in the garden, even to the extent of growing plants and vegetables that will produce decorative seedheads or beanpods.

Children enjoy making this kind of mosaic and an example will be given of one made by the children of Cottenham Village College.

135 Seeds and beans being heated in oven

136 Pans of seeds and beans

The general method of preparing the material for these mosaics is first to choose a varied quantity of seeds, beans, etc., separating those which will germinate or form a mould. These must be spread on an oven tray and heated for 15 minutes or so in the oven at a temperature of 350°. They should be left to cool and then sorted into glass jars—jam jars or kilner depending on size and quantity—and stored in a dry place. They will look very decorative on open shelves (135, 136).

Bark is another material that combines well with seeds, or it can equally well be used alone. Choose as many varieties and shapes as possible with an eye to the different tones of colour that can be found. Willow is a greyish silver, while walnut and chestnut have browner tones, and some of the conifers have shades of copper red. Many of these barks have greenish markings of lichen and moss and though most of this will disappear when baked in the oven, sometimes a tinge of it remains.

As with the seeds it is equally important to bake the barks, as many of them harbour woodlice, and most of them need drying out before any adhesive can be applied.

Bark can often be collected from around the base of the tree or on the ground. If it has to be stripped off it is usually possible to find a piece that is loose that can be prised off easily. Some trees present long rectangular slithers, while others shed their bark in shorter sections.

When you are designing a mosaic with bark, never attempt to cut it or shape it, but break off sections along the natural cracks and allow the natural form to compose the design. It is, in fact, quite difficult to go wrong with the design of a bark mosaic.

The only equipment necessary is a pair of tweezers (if tiny seeds are being used) and a spatula or length of stiff cardboard for spreading the adhesive.

EXAMPLE 1

Village College seed mosaic

The idea for the pattern of this came from photographs of snakes and snake skins. A large picture of snakes coiled up and intertwined gave the original idea of composition and various freehand drawing was done until a pattern was evolved that pleased everyone.

This was drawn on to the board with charcoal by the children (average age 12 years), nine of them working on it at a time.

Materials

Assorted seeds including beans, peas, wheat, melon seeds
Evostick and *Copydex* adhesive
Hardboard, battened at the back for rigidity (3′ × 4′)
Cardboard spatulas for spreading adhesive

Method of working

The seeds were laid on to the drawn design on the hardboard, which was used on the rough side. Small areas of adhesive were spread at a time and the larger beans and seeds placed singly by hand. The smaller ones were spread in small handfuls and by hand gently smoothed across the adhesive. As a general rule the larger beans outlined the main forms, while the small ones were used to fill in the background.

The colours were white, chocolate brown, silvery green, and purple flecked with white (runner beans) with a few touches of greenish yellow brought in by the broad beans.

The illustrations will show the method of working and the final mosaic which was proudly set up on the walls of the class room (137, 138, 139).

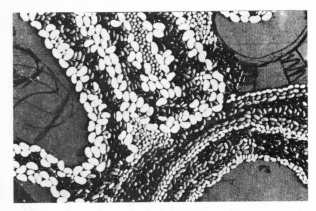

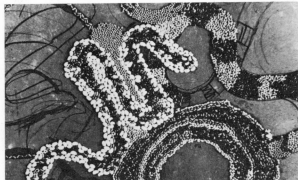

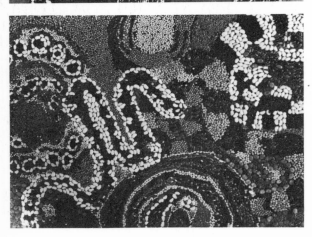

137 Detail of children's mosaic

138 Detail of children's mosaic

EXAMPLE 2

Woodpecker mosaic (141)

This design was sketched on to hardboard with black chalk and composed mainly of chocolate black coffee beans, broad beans, lima beans and French beans. The background was deliberately kept varied in the colour and size of the beans to add liveliness.

Materials

> Assorted beans
> *Unibond* adhesive
> Hardboard $12'' \times 12''$ (rough side used)
> Oak framing $1'' \times \frac{1}{8}''$

Method of working

This was almost exactly that used in the Village College mosaic except that a rather thicker skin of adhesive was used to offset the oily surface of the coffee beans, which made them more difficult to stick down.

A final rather important point to stress when making seed and bean mosaics. Keep them away from mice! If they are stored away in a disused shed or a barn they provide the ideal winter feast for hungry vermin. Indeed, a seed mosaic made by the author was completely devoured in the course of one short week leaving only the husks of the seeds and the chalk lines of the design!

139 Final of children's mosaic

140 Mixed natural materials in random design
141 Woodpecker mosaic

EXAMPLE 3

Bark and seed mosaic

Most of the materials used in this mosaic picture were collected in the countryside with the exception of a few of the beans which were bought at a grocer's —the coffee beans, the white butter beans and the dried peas. The wood panel that served as a base was an old disused drawing board that seemed to have a sympathetic quality in its grain and, indeed, although it was completely covered up in the end, the patterning of the grain served largely to inspire the design (140).

A random type of design seems the best to choose for this kind of medium, perhaps one that is vaguely reminiscent of the rolling hills, waving fields of corn, the wandering line of a brook and the occasional tall uprights of the trees. The textures used can echo this idea—the roughness of the bark with its broken uneven contours, the areas of strewn grain, smooth-sided stones and the many-surfaced seeds and beans.

The design was sketchily laid out and then viewed through a reducing glass (or the wrong end of field glasses) with frequent alterations of the various masses until the right kind of pattern seemed to emerge. None of the areas was glued down until the whole became a satisfactory design, although quite a few alterations were made as the work progressed and the idea become clearer.

142 Plastic mortar spread into bark concavity

Materials

A plywood board $1/2''$ thick
$1/4$ pint tin *Unibond*
$1/2$ lb *Nic-o-Bond Thikbed*
Bark from willow, elm, chestnut and walnut
The following beans and seeds (quantities approximate)
$1/4$ lb butter beans
$1/2$ dozen broad beans
$1/4$ lb dried peas
$1/4$ lb coffee beans (dark roast)
2 ozs of three varieties of french beans (white, brown and purplish-black)
2 ozs runner beans (purple and black flecked)
A few melon and pumpkin seeds, a mixture of wheat, oats, rice, mustard and spinach seeds
A few white pebbles
Tools
A palette knife (for spreading the glue)
A thin pointed vegetable knife
Tweezers (generally necessary but not used for this work)

Method of working

The method of designing this work has already been discussed. The various materials were collected and selected, although it is a good idea to keep a fairly varied stock of bean seeds, stones, etc., for this type of mosaic. Even bark can be collected in any season and stored for a considerable time. Where there is any possibility of germination, the seeds and beans should, as stated before, be baked in an oven, although this often affects the colour. Bark should certainly be baked to discourage weevils, woodlice, and to prevent the formation of moulds.

STEP 1

The larger masses, such as the bark, were first out-lined with white chalk. As many of the strips of bark were twisted or concave it was necessary to trowel a layer of plastic mortar *(Nic-o-Bond Thikbed)* into the cavities so that they could lie flat on the board (142). When the baseboard itself is rather porous it may be necessary to apply a coat of fast-setting glue such as *Unibond* to the flat surface of the *Nic-o-Bond* when it has set hard.

STEP 2

The areas between the bark were now lightly sketch-ed in with the chalk, often carrying the different textured areas across and beyond the bark so that the background became a unified mass and not just small areas filled in with different material. The col-our, shapes and different surface textures (i.e. matt, glossy, rough, sharp or rounded) were carefully considered and placed in what seemed a right rela-tionship to each other. As mentioned earlier, the unfolding pattern was constantly reviewed by peer-ing at it through the wrong end of field glasses (or opera glasses).

STEP 3

The glue *(Unibond)* was applied when the areas were sketched in, covering only small sections at a time, owing to the fast drying nature of the glue. This type of glue has the advantage of drying completely transparent, so that though it may be difficult to apply it neatly at first, it is reassuring to know that it will dry quite invisibly. Where it had been decided beforehand which seeds and beans were to be used in certain areas, a single sample was glued on first to see if it looked right, before the general glueing was done. Quite frequently, though, one gets the feeling of what is right as the work progresses. Some people find that the better method is to cover all the sur-faces with the material before glueing any of it down and then more radical changes can be made before one is finally committed.

In this mosaic the darker material was mainly on the edges to act as the suggestion of a frame by clearly defining the edges. Coffee beans were used here with a few shiny black dwarf beans. Owing to their oily nature the coffee beans were very difficult to stick with any permanency and several rolled off when the work was moved for the photograph. They have a deep rich glow which no other bean has and seemed ideal for this mosaic, but on the whole would be better avoided for technical reasons. Final mosaic fig. 143.

STEP 4

The final step in this relatively simple mosaic was to frame it suitably in natural wood. It is often con-sidered necessary to varnish the beans and seeds on this type of work and sometimes they are sprayed with cellulose, but in this case the lively textures of the differing materials seemed better left alone as nature had made them.

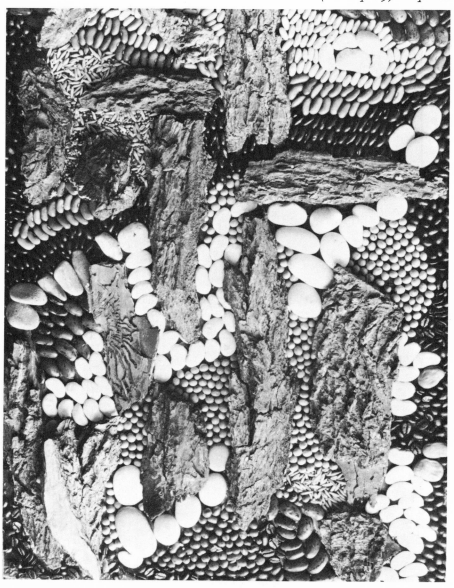

Another type of material which is available to everyone is wood in its many forms and textures. It is a sympathetic medium that may be used in large scale outdoor projects where it will mellow and weather to become an integral part of the natural scene, or as a more geometric mural indoors where it is sawn into small sections and used as tesserae.

For the outdoor mural or background to a patio it is better used in its original texture and colour, sawn only to workable sized units which can be as large or small as the situation demands. Indoors it may be used stained, or painted and sanded down again (gloss painted areas of wood are seldom successful), or simply in its natural tone and finish, although interesting mosaics have been made from unfinished softwood and highly polished veneers.

Timber merchants and sawmills always have a plentiful supply of waste sections of wood and will generally allow you to fill a small box with what you may require, free of cost. If, however, you plan to use different shaped sections such as triangles, or circles, it is best to buy lengths of the wood and cut thin sections from these, or get a jobbing carpenter to do this for you. A small power saw is the tool to use for this, as hand sawing is far too laborious and leaves the edges very rough.

An adhesive such as *Unibond, Evostick,* or *Bondcrete* is generally used. If a rather thick base is required to bed down awkward shapes, sand can be mixed in small quantities with the adhesive alone or the adhesive added to a cement mix. As wood does not bond to cement, a good deal of adhesive should be added.

The wood mosaic shown (144, 145) and described in the following example should give a broad idea of the method that many be used for most wood mosaics.

EXAMPLE

Materials

A wooden broom handle 1″ diameter, cut into 1/8″ sections
A wooden dowel stick 1/2″ diameter, cut into 1/8″ sections
1′ length 1″ × 1″ softwood, cut into 1″ sections
1′ length 1″ × 1/8″ softwood, cut into 1″ sections
Several rectangles of 1″ × 1/2″ oak, cut into 2″ lengths
2 squares of 3″ × 1/4″ oak
A blockboard baseboard 18″ × 10″ × 1/4″
Evostick adhesive

Method of designing

This was purposely confined to a few suggested lines, and as the wood pieces were brought on to the design it was altered considerably and the wood itself dictated the final mosaic.

Method of working

The wood sections were sandpapered down until the edges were smooth and all projecting splinters removed. The shapes were sorted into boxes and

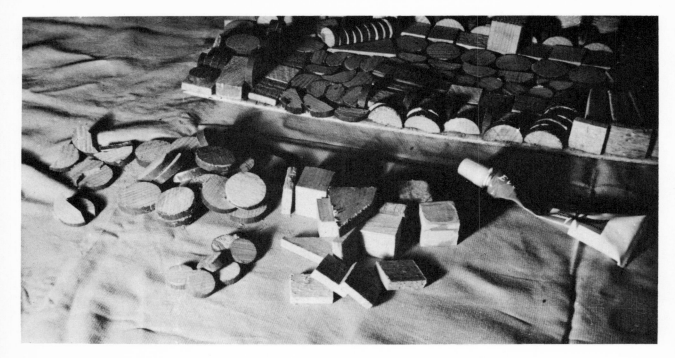

144 Materials being assembled

about one-third of the broomstick circles were split in half with a sharp chisel to form half circles.

Before the wood was glued on to the baseboard, certain sections of circles were glued together to form curved piles that would be finally laid down sideways, 'top hats' were glued together to be laid later on the 3″ × 3″ squares, but most of the wood was glued directly on to the baseboard. Extra glue was added to vertical sides that came in contact with each other, for extra strength.

Most of the mosaic was done in one evening and left to dry, a few final touches being added on the following morning.

This work was done by a boy of 12 and although some guide lines were drawn in on the baseboard, the majority of these were ignored and the final

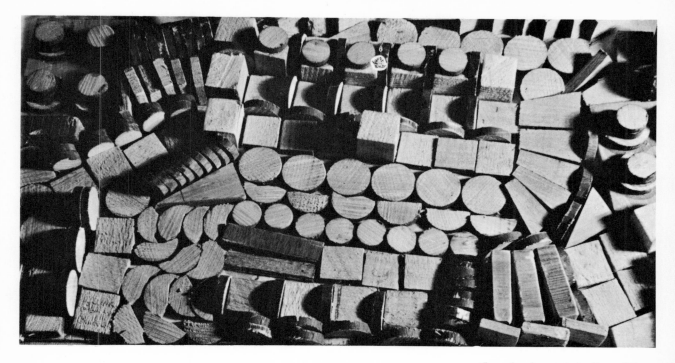

145 Completed mosaic by Peter Hutton

design was almost entirely his own idea of massing and grouping the small units into regimented areas.

Many variations on this type of mosaic will come to mind. The background can be painted in a deep rich colour such as prussian blue and the wood forms will be thrown into strong relief. Certain areas of the background can be painted in different colours, or stained with a wood dye. The sides of the wood sec-

tions can be painted or stained before being sawn. This latter will give a suggestion of colour to the edges only.

Larger wood sections to be used on more ambitious projects such as a mosaic mural, can have the surface sanded into texture patterns and paint or stain worked over the areas by lightly brushing and sanding down again.

Schools and Group
Mosaics   X

Most children will readily accept mosaic making as one of the most fascinating occupations, and are generally eager to collect and bring a great variety of material to use in their designs, often inspiring their parents or teachers with a degree of their enthusiasm.

In the case of small children, it is obviously better to limit the materials to those which can be handled with safety, avoiding glass or sharp-edged tesserae, but with older children or groups of adults, anything may be used that will combine into a harmoniously balanced design.

Many schools and technical colleges and even night schools now have facilities for firing their own tesserae, and a supply of these should be built up to provide sufficient variety for all purposes. It is possible to salvage quite a large proportion of tesserae from projects that have been unsuccessful by simply breaking up the mortar from behind with a hammer and re-using the tesserae. For experimental work it is usually better to have a mortar like *Sirapite* or *Polyfilla,* than a more permanent cement bonded one. Other, more fragile kinds of tesserae are shells, buttons, seeds and beans, broken china, tiles, marbles, bark or sections of fish backbone or wood.

Designing is generally better left to children to work out alone, throwing in a few suggestions if inspiration fails. But this is seldom necessary. Adults often require a starting point for a large-scale mural on which several people may work together and some suggestions and ideas are given in chapter I.

Children will sometimes prefer a figurative design, and may enjoy working out their own interpretations of the kings and queens of England, the Canterbury pilgrims, or their own street, to set in panels as a long mosaic mural. A mosaic of this type is being done by the children of Cottenham Village College; the first panel is illustrated (146, 148, 149). The design chosen was an aerial plan of the village.

Two methods of group working are suggested. Individual sections of a large-scale mosaic may be designed by different people participating and carried out individually by them, or a complete mosaic is designed by one person to be worked on sectionally by the group. Either the Direct or the Reverse method may be employed for both approaches, although individually designed sections have more vitality if the tesserae are set in by hand and the whole interpretation carried through by the same person.

Working as a group is an excellent way of making pebble pavements, each member contributing a plaque of a different design in the same type of pebble so that the unity will be maintained.

Several examples are shown of various projects done by children of Cottenham Village College, Cambridge.

CERAMIC TESSERAE MOSAIC MURAL

The examples shown (146, 148, 149) are of one panel in a large mosaic being carried out by the children of Cottenham Village College, Cambridge, for an exterior wall of their school building. Each unit has been designed to be successful in its own right as well as a part of the whole mural.

Materials

Hand-made tesserae in many shapes, sizes, and colours
Pebbles and stones
Marbles
Asbestos units (2′×2′) as backing boards
Cement mortar of 1 part cement to 3 parts sand
Wood for framework

Size

Overall 6′×16′ divided into 8 panels of 2′×6′. Each working unit being 2′×2′. This to be attached to the wall into a previously built-in framework.

Method of working

The tesserae were made and fired according to the method described in chapter V. Children working on this project are illustrated (147). The design decided upon—an aerial plan of the village—was enlarged from the original sketch onto the 2′×2′ asbestos units by transferring the design on to the wet mortar with a sharp stick and placing the tesserae into this by the Direct method. The picture shows a completed unit (146).

146 Unit of mosaic mural, laid out

147 Children in stages of tesserae making

148 Sections of unit—side view

149 Sections of unit—front view

When three sections are ready, they will be placed into the framework, one lying on top of the other. The next panel is to be done the same way until all eight panels are completed. These panels could be removed at a later date to be replaced by another mosaic made by a different group of children.

All the mosaics made by the children of Cottenham Village College were done under the direction of the art teacher, Miss Kate Varney.

Although all the work described in this chapter has been done by children of two age groups, the same type of projects could be undertaken by a family in a joint effort, arranging that the simple areas are to be done by the youngest members of the group and the more complicated parts by the older children or the parents. The wall or the pavement of a patio decorated in such a manner would provide a summer entertainment while the surround to a bathroom or a paper mosaic along a playroom wall could occupy the winter days. Each member of the family or group could choose some form or symbol for their unit, such as a star, a sun, a wheel, a fish or perhaps an eye, simple shapes for the youngest or less adventurous.

The materials used need not be expensive tesserae but the many natural objects found on the shores and countryside, shown in many examples in this book.

150 Cockerel in oyster shells and bark

COCK MADE IN BARK AND OYSTER SHELLS (150)

This is an example of a figurative representation designed and carried out by 11 year old children.

The bark was broken by hand into the many natural shapes that were ideally suited to the subject, the brown, rough texture of the bark. It was glued onto hardboard with a quick-drying plastic glue.

PAPER MOSAIC

This was designed and made by children in the 12 to 13 age group, as a mural for the wall of the art room, the size being 19′ × 4′.

Method of designing

Various natural forms were considered and discussed with the children—the cell forms in the felled section of an old tree, cross sections of onions or cabbage, ripples across water, a fish skeleton, a butterfly's wing. Individual interpretations of most of these motifs were drawn out by each child and small trial mosaics were made before the larger one was attempted. Working in groups of four, the children then chose which of the designs would be carried out on the large-scale mosaic. The felled tree section was finally selected and some children worked on the whole spiral motif while others chose to work on a section of it.

Method of working

The children stood round a large trestle table in the same groups of four. They were given sheets of white sugar paper about 4′ × 4′ in area and a limited range of coloured paper (in this case chosen by the teacher), the aim being to give a unity to the overall mosaic. The colours were black, white, dark grey, golden brown and silver and large quantities of these shades were cut on the school guillotine by the teacher so that the tesserae would be kept to simple shapes (scissors can be used, of course). It should be noted, as can be seen from the illustrations (151-4) that quite a diversity of shapes could be cut in the rectangular form and this fact has contributed to the liveliness and interest of the patterns. The paper tesserae were brushed with a flour and water paste (cellulose wallpaper paste may be used) and applied along the design lines drawn on the 4′ × 4′ paper sections.

When all of these were completed, they were assembled by the children who had attempted to make the lines in the different sections link by frequently matching them together while working. Apart from the practical aspect of designing in sections, the division lines provide a pleasant discipline to a design that otherwise might prove too complex, added to the fact that the children might find difficulty in designing such a large area and envisaging the final overall effect.

The separate large sections were placed on a pinboard, *in situ,* and it was found that several variations of the whole mosaic could be made by changing the different sections.

151 Materials for paper mosaics

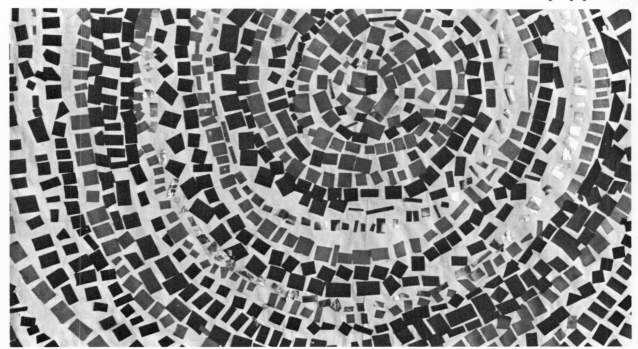

152 Section of paper mosaic

153 Two units of paper mosaic

154 Completed paper mosaic

124

SEED MASKS (155, 156, 157)

Seeds were the mosaic medium used for these seed masks and the design idea was based on African masks seen by one of the children who also contributed a fine supply of dried red berries.

The base of papier mâché was first made by tearing up quantities of newspaper, brushing the torn pieces with an ordinary flour and water paste and sticking them in layers onto an oval plaster mould (made by the method described for a plaster batt on page 127). Many layers were pasted in this way, each one being allowed to dry before the next one was applied, the whole process taking a week. The holes for the eyes were cut out with a sharp knife when the papier mâché form was dry and hard.

The pattern areas were outlined on to the masks with charcoal and the seeds and beans selected for each design. The basic ones used were broad beans, purple dwarf beans, dried peas, haricot beans and dried vermilion berries. These were glued onto the masks with a quick drying plastic adhesive, working in several different stages.

155 A seed mask half finished

156 A completed mask

157 Three seed masks in progress

The final illustration (158) is of a mosaic in ging-ham and rag, designed to stumulate the children's ideas for working in more permanent tesserae media.

158 Mosaic in gingham and rag

Several of these recipes for mortar mixes are to be found in the chapters to which they are relevant, but it may be useful to give a general summary of all of them here for easy reference, together with a brief description of some of the commercial adhesives and their properties.

The basic materials for mortar mixes are generally sand and cement.

Portland cement   This may be bought from any builders' merchant and is usually sold in hundred-weight bags. It can be obtained in smaller quantities although it is seldom worth buying less than 14 lbs. This is generally sufficient for the mosaic artist as it has to be used while reasonably fresh, and *must* be kept dry and frost-proof or it will go off (lose its setting properties); so it is better to buy in small quantities rather than to waste half a hundredweight sack.

Sand   is also obtained from the builders' merchants and comes in two grades, silver sand and sharp sand. It must be kept dry and never used damp in a cement mix.

Hydrated lime   In addition to making the mortar more workable, a small percentage added to the mix delays the setting time.

Ciment fondu   A dark grey cement, more expensive than Portland. It creates a stronger bond, sets more rapidly and is static, i.e. does not shrink or swell. It is often used when a strong bonding mortar is required such as slab glass cement mosaics.

Cementone is a commercial colouring for all cement mixes. It comes in several shades, all of which are permanent. It is limeproof and stated by the manufacturers to be fadeless.

Sirapite   The proprietary name for a quick harden-ing plaster. It is pink in colour but may be tinted with *Cementone*. It is very useful for small mosaics or work in schools as it is fairly cheap, but is unsuitable for exterior mosaics.

Polyfilla   A similar quick hardening plaster, white in colour but rather more expensive, as it is only sold in packets.

MORTAR MIXES, CARPENTRY

So many adhesives are now on the market—poly-vinyl acetate resins, casein glues (some of which may not be water-resistant), plastic cements—most of which may be used for mosaics, but for the purpose of this book it is better to confine the choice to a few that have been personally used. Their trade names are given here.

Bondcrete and *Unibond* are excellent for all types of mosaics where an adhesive method is used. They are waterproof and easy to apply and may be the base for the Direct method when a mortar setting bed is not being used.

Evostik, Fixtite and *Richafix* are similar adhesives. *Bondcrete* and *Unibond* are used in small quantities to make a cement-mix bond on to glass and ceramics more firmly.

There are also ready-mixed grouts such as *Poly-grout* and *Nic-o-Grout*. *Nic-o-Bond Thikbed* is a cement-mix of more substance which makes an excellent setting bed for tesserae of all thicknesses. It takes two to three hours to set.

Araldite is an epoxy resin glue which sets intensely hard and is usually employed to bond sheets of glass together for mosaic making. *Tensol* is also used for this purpose.

Basic mortar recipe (see Direct method procedure, chapter III)
  3 parts sharp sand
  1 part Portland cement
  1/8 part hydrated lime
  Mix fairly dry

Grout recipe (chapter IV, the Owl Mosaic)
  8 parts fine sand
  2 parts cement
  1 part hydrated lime
  Mix to the consistency of thick syrup.

Grout recipe (for filling papered sections (Reverse method) or grouting direct laid tesserae)
  5 parts Portland cement
  1 part lime
  Mix to the consistency of cream and spread over the mosaic, working well into the cracks.

Foundation mortar (for pavement laying)
  4 parts sharp sand
  4 parts 1/2″ gravel
  1 part Portland cement
  This should be laid to a depth of 1 1/2″.

Mortar recipe (for bedding pavement units and filling between)

  10 parts sharp sand
  2 parts hydrated lime
  1 part Portland cement
  This mix should not be too dry.

Putty for glass mosaics (translucent type, chapter VI)
  3 parts whiting
  1 part *Sirapite* (or plaster of Paris)
  Lamp-black powder to mix to a dark grey-black
  Linseed oil to mix to a dryish paste
  Turpentine (sufficient to further moisten to consistency of putty)
  This putty is worked into the cracks between the tesserae.

To mix plaster of Paris (for plaster batts, etc.)
  For a hard mould
  The plaster is mixed by adding it to water at room temperature and *never* by pouring water on to it.
  18 parts of plaster to 9 of water

For a simpler method, without any measuring, half fill a bucket of water and add handfuls of plaster until the water is saturated and a small mound of dry plaster rises above the water, disappearing after a few moments. The mixture should then be mixed slowly by hand or with a wooden stick, allowing no bubbles to form, until it is of an even consistency. Pour this into a wooden frame if required for a batt. Clean bucket immediately.

PREPARING NEWLY-DUG CLAY

Collect a quantity of clay and place in buckets of water for moistening. Press the slopped-down clay through a fine 80 mesh sieve several times with the help of stiff brushes. Siphon off water until clay is workable. It should be stored for maturing and then subjected to further treatment of kneading by hand. It must be worked in this way until it is homogeneous and free from air bubbles.

WATERPROOFING

Water glass brushed over chipboard of 1/2″ plywood (thinner wood will warp unless battened) in a fairly strong solution is an adequate means of waterproofing backing boards for mosaic. Shellac can also be used for this purpose.

WOODEN FRAME FOR SETTING MORTAR IN (159)

For the average small mosaic a frame made of 2″ × 1″ plain softwood is suitable. This simple frame is hinged at one corner and fixed with a small hook and eye at the opposite corner. This makes it possible to open the whole frame outwards after the mosaic has been finished without disturbing the edge of the cement or plaster base. The larger mosaics will need more substantial wooden framing, as the essential thing is that the wood shall not bend when the plaster is pressed down into the frame.

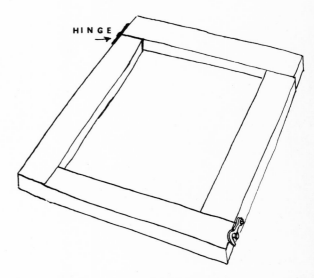

HINGE

159 Wooden frame for setting mortar

FLOUR AND WATER PASTE

Combine 1 oz flour with 1 gill water and mix to a smooth paste. Bring to boil and boil for five minutes, stirring constantly to avoid lumps. Cool and use to stick tessera on to paper for the Reverse method. The paper is easily removable when damped.

Bibliography

Billington, Dora, *The Technique of Pottery,* B.T. Batsford Ltd, London

Damaz, Paul, *Art in European Architecture,* Reinhold Publishing Corporation, New York

Ellis, Clarence, *The Pebbles on the Beach,* Faber & Faber Ltd, London

Hendrickson, Edwin, *Mosaics, Hobby and Art,* Cornerstone Library, New York

Jenkins and Mills, *The Art of Making Mosaics,* Van Nostrand, Princeton, New Jersey

Lauppi, Walter, *Stein an Stein,* Verlag Paul Haupt, Bern, Switzerland

Lee Aller, Doris and Diane, *Mosaics,* Lane Book Co, California

Petas, Frantisek, *Medieval Mosaic,* Spring Books, London

Rada, P., *Book of Ceramics,* Spring Books, London

Röttger, Ernst, *Creative Clay Craft,* B.T. Batsford Ltd, London

Saunders, Herbert H., *Practical Pottery Book,* Blandford Press, London

Steers, J.A., *The Coastline of England and Wales,* Cambridge University Press

Strache, Wolf, *Forms and Patterns in Nature,* Pantheon Books, New York

Whitmore, Thomas, *The Mosaics of Hagia Sophia at Istanbul,* Byzantine Institute, Oxford University Press, London

Williamson, Robert, *Mosaics,* Crosby Lockwood, London

Aggregate – An additive to concrete, generally in the form of gravel or granite

Biscuit firing – Preliminary low-temperature firing of the clay

Cartoon – The full-scale drawing, from which the final work is done

Ceramic – Clay which has been glazed and fired, generally having a coloured face

Chinagraph pencil – A wax pencil used for drawing on glass or glazed surfaces

Chipboard – A cheaper and heavier form of plywood with a centre filling of wood particles bound together with glue

Contour line – Line of direction taken by tesserae to describe form

Corbelling – Building out of brickwork to form a ledge of support

Encaustic tiles – Tiles in which the pigment is incorporated in the clay and not merely painted on the surface before firing

Expanded metal – A form of metal mesh for reinforcing concrete

Figurative and non-figurative – Figurative art seeks to depict the thing seen. Non-figurative art deals with abstractions

Filato – Minute glass rods cut in sections and used in small-scale mosaic jewellery

Fissile – A fissile mineral is one which splits fairly easily

Flashed glass – Glass in which colour is fused on to one surface only

Flint – An additive to the clay body

Flint knapping – The traditional craft of splitting and cutting flints

Glaze – A glass-like layer covering the surface of ceramic

Grout – A thin mortar used to fill the cracks between tesserae

Half drop – A staggered repeat of pattern (see fig. 2)

Kiln wash – A substance to protect the kiln shelves against running glazes

Knocking up – The kneading of clay to prepare it for firing

Lead bisicilicate – A form of lead which has been rendered non-poisonous by firing

Leather dry – Partially dry clay which can still take an impression

Light box – A wooden framework, about 2″ × 3″ over which a sheet of 32 oz frosted glass is laid to cover a strip light. For viewing the colours of stained glass

Linear design – Design of which the main part is line, or edge

Maquette – Small-scale model of the project

Monochromatic – Being of shades of one colour

Negative pattern – The shapes left between motifs

Reducing glass – A concave glass which acts in the opposite manner from a magnifying glass

Seger cone – Ceramic cones, numbered and marked at exact temperatures at which the tops bend in a kiln

Sgraffito – The scratching of a design either lightly or deeply on to the surface of the clay

Slip – Basically a liquid solution of the clay used in the body of the work which can have additions or colour added. It is painted or poured on to the surface before firing

Smalti – The name given to the tesserae which were used for traditional mosaics, manufactured in Italy

Tungsten lighting – Normal domestic light bulbs

List of Suppliers in Great Britain

CERAMICS

British Ceramic Service Co. Ltd, 1 Park Avenue, Wolstanton, Newcastle, Staffs
Kilns, kiln furniture, clay, glazes, slips, etc.
Fulham Pottery Ltd, 210 New Kings Road, London S.W.6
Clays, glazes, kilns, etc.
Podmore and Co. Ltd, Caledonian Mill, Shelton, Stoke-on-Trent, Staffs
Kilns, kiln furniture, clay, glazes, slips, all necessary equipment
Webcot Ltd, Alfred Street, Fenton, Stoke-on-Trent, Staffs
Kilns, kiln furniture, clay, glazes, slips, etc.

MORTARS AND ADHESIVES

Ciba Ltd, Duxford, Cambridge
Araldite adhesives and epoxy resins
Joseph Freeman and Sons Ltd, 96 Garratt Lane, London S.W.18
Cementone products
Nicholls and Clarke Ltd, Shoreditch High Street, London E.1
Nic-o-Bond Thikbed and tile cement
Richard Tiles Ltd, Tunstall, Stoke-on-Trent, Staffs
Richafix adhesive, tiles and mosaics
Unibond adhesive

Bondcrete adhesive Most builders' merchants
Evostik adhesive
All builders' merchants supply concrete, ciment fondu, *Sirapite,* lime and sand

STAINED GLASS

James Hetley and Co. Ltd, Beresford Avenue, Wembley, Middlesex
Stained glass of all types, slab glass

TESSERAE

Bush Crafts Ltd, 25–27 Bramley Road, London W.8 (Most mosaic materials). Wood panels, table legs, squared paper, gummed mosaic paper, Byzantine smalti mosaic for murals, smalti mosaic—thin strips, *Saivo* Italian glass mosaic, *Mosacol* cement, cutters
Proctor and Lavender Mosaics, Solihull, Warwickshire
Kosta glass mosaic (Swedish), squares ($3/4'' \times 3/4''$), oblongs ($3/4'' \times 1 1/2''$)
Edgar Udney and Co. Ltd.
(Most mosaic materials). Vitreous, glazed and unglazed ceramics, smalti, marble pieces, cubes, mosaic paper, gum, setting trays, hammers, cutters, *Mosicfix* adhesive, *Fixtite*

For the benefit of American readers the following is a list of pebbles to be found on coastal stretches of the U.S.A. It is by no means comprehensive and for information on Canada a series of booklets is available issued by the Geological Survey of Canada (Department of Mines and Technical Surveys, Ottawa) Volumes 1, 2, and 3.

California

San Diego, Imperial Beach
Moss agates, varied pebbles
Long Beach
Dolomite, gypsum, agates, quartz crystals
Renondo Beach
Moonstone, jasper, agates
Conquina Beach
Fossil shells
Santa Barbara to Jalama Beach
Whalebone, petrified wood, jasper, agate pebbles, marcasite nubules
Gorda area
Jade, nephrite jade, jasper
Trinidad
Carnelian, californite, jasper

Oregon

Port Oxford
Agatized coral

Newport (best beach collecting areas on the coast)
Garnet, fossil wood, agates, jasper
Yachats (best beach collecting areas on the coast)
Every Variety of agate, sagenite, moss iris, marcasite, jasper, wood, bloodstone (best collected after winter storms)

Washington

Wallapa Bay
Agate, jasper, chalcedony

Port Orford

Agatized coral

Yachats

Every variety agate, marcasite, jasper, bloodstone (best collected after winter storms)

Washington

Willapa Bay
Agate, jasper, chalcedony
Maclips
Chalcedony, agate, jasper, clear quartz
Lopush
Jasper, chalcedony, spherulitic jasper
Agate Bay
Jasper pebbles

List of Suppliers in the USA

Most of these firms will send mail orders to any part of the U.S.A.

Mosaic Crafts Inc., 80 West 3rd Street, (nr 6th Avenue), New York City

Vedovato Brothers Inc., 246 East 116 Street, New York City

Dillon Tile Co., 252 12th Street, San Francisco, California

American Mosaic Co., 912 First Street NW, Washington D C

Gager's Handicraft, 1024 Nicollet Avenue, Minneapolis, Minnesota

Ravenna Mosaic Co., 3126 Nebraska, St Louis, Missouri

Suppliers of Magnesite (mortar)

Berkshire Chemicals Inc., 155 East 44th Street, New York City

Kaiser Aluminium Chemical Sales Inc., 300 Lakeside Drive, Oakland, California

List of Suppliers in Australia

Glazes and kilns

H. B. Selby and Co. Pty Ltd, 393 Swanston Street, Melbourne, Victoria, (also addresses in Sydney, Adelaide, Brisbane, Hobart, Perth. See local directories)

Ceramic and glass mosaic, smalti, ceramic tiles

W. M. Crosby (Merchandise) Pty Ltd, 266–274 King Street, Melbourne (also at Hobart, Launceston, Perth, Sydney, Brisbane, Adelaide. See local directories)

Ceramic raw materials, potting clays

Rodda Pty Ltd, 62 Beach Street, Port Melbourne, Victoria. Agents in all states and also in New Zealand. Sole Australian Agents for Pike Brothers: Fayle and Co Ltd, producers of Dorset ball clay

Pottery clays, ceramic glazes and American 'Tru-Fyre' ceramic glazes

Camden Art Centre Pty Ltd, 188–200 Gertrude Street, Fitzroy, N. 6. Victoria

Index

1357